When You
Need a Lift

When You
Need a Lift

But Don't Want to Eat Chocolate,
Pay a Shrink, or Drink a Bottle of Gin

Joy Behar and Friends

Crown Publishers
New York

Library of Congress Cataloging-in-Publication Data

When you need a lift : but don't want to eat chocolate, pay a
shrink, or drink a bottle of gin / Joy Behar and friends.—1st ed.
1. Conduct of life—Quotations, maxims, etc. I. Behar, Joy. II. Title.

PN6084.C556W494 2007
818'.602—dc22   2007010067

ISBN 978-0-307-35171-5

Printed in the United States of America

10 9 8 7 6 5 4 3 2 1

First Edition

Contents

v

Introduction

Joy Behar

Just reading the front page of the newspaper these days is enough to put even the relentlessly cheerful von Trapp family into a serious state of melancholy. Maybe the world has always been riddled with disasters and misery, but that doesn't mean that I can't enjoy a double mocha latte with whipped cream. Too fattening, you say. I agree. It's getting more and more difficult to eat my way out of my mood swings.

When I was a child, my mother would get into a funk over things that I didn't understand, but I noticed that she could always snap herself out of it by putting on an aria from *Madama Butterfly*. The next thing I knew, she'd be singing along and having a wonderful time, even though she was crying for poor Butterfly. It was her way of cheering herself up. I realized then that it was up to me to monitor my ups and downs, and her opera collection.

These days, when the doldrums hit, I head for a department store. I find that loitering near the handbags has a calming effect on me. The smell of a Gucci bag is like a trip to Siena in June.

My second-favorite mood elevator is a manicure and pedicure, with a neck massage thrown in. Lately, I've discovered that the little nail salons that are popping up all over the city where I live offer a reflexology treatment between pedicures. I think I'll just move into one these shops.

If all else fails, I get on the phone with my girlfriends and start marathon blabbing. After two or three hours of nonstop analysis of our issues, I feel completely liberated from any threat of the blues.

In the spirit of group participation, I've asked a hundred and one of my friends, associates, and role models what they do when they're feeling down. I'm happy to say that their responses have been as varied and helpful as they have been interesting and original.

This is not a "how-to" book. I don't like how-to books. Just because Dr. So-and-So does it one way does not mean that I'm going to want to do it that way. I like to get a variety of answers on the big questions in life. Sigmund Freud was smart and probably right about a lot of things, but "penis envy"? I don't think so.

So, when you're in the doldrums and a hot fudge sundae isn't doing it for you, check out this book. Not everyone's ideas will appeal to you. If repeating a mantra makes you anxious, don't meditate. Personally, I find fishing tedious, but if that's your hook, go for it.

And by all means, stay away from anything that Sylvia Plath wrote.

A

Patch Adams

In this world, I think a person can choose who he or she wishes to be, becoming a composition of intentions. Deciding to be happy, I only had to determine the ideal performance to forward my intentions, then notice the resulting consequences. I left living in a syntax of "because" (because I'm too old, I have cancer, of what my father did, I'm shy, etc.) and switched to a syntax of "so that" (I do this . . . so that my intention is put forward). It is what Buddhists call "mindfulness," to be present and involved in making me.

The human world is so close to its own extinction that we don't have time to invest in feeling miserable; it is a self-centered act that stands in the way. Do for others in care, and your down day turns to bright sunshine. Throw away your tablets and be enchanting! Whee!

Patch Adams is a medical doctor, clown, performer, and social activist. In 1971, he founded the Gesundheit! Institute, a holistic medical community that has provided free medical care to thousands. He is the author of two books, *Gesundheit!* and *House Calls*, and is the subject of a major motion picture starring Robin Williams titled *Patch Adams.*

David A. Adler

I'm a writer, so being tired or in a bad mood can mean I'll lose a day's work. I have lots of deadlines, so I simply cannot afford bad moods. And, of course, they're no fun.

Talking to friends always improves my mood. If I call you to talk, it could be that talking to you makes me feel good. I have also filled my office with things that cheer me: lots of books, family photographs, good-smelling citrus plants, and tapes of radio programs from the 1930s and '40s—you know the ones, *Fibber McGee and Molly, Lux Radio Theater, The Jack Benny Show, The Whistler,* and *The Bickersons.* I also have several models of cars from my youth, a 1962 Chevy Bel Air (my first car), a 1950 Hudson, and a 1965 Pontiac GTO, among others. You wondered what child would want those toys. Well, I'm that child! Whenever I buy a new toy, I tell myself it's cheaper than a session with a psychologist or medication.

Just entering my office cheers me. It's my place. I think it's great to have a "happy space," and I feel fortunate that mine is where I spend many hours each day working.

David A. Adler is the author of more than two hundred books for young readers, including the Cam Jansen mysteries, the Picture Book Biography series, the Andy Russell books, and *The Babe and I.*

Brian W. Aldiss

There are many people I love, many I enjoy, many for whom I am grateful.

Nevertheless, I cannot but feel that humanity as a whole is a bit of a flop. We have overrun the planet like a form of pest and are busy ruining it. Even the permafrost in Siberia is melting.

All these things make one feel bad. And bad is what we should feel. It's not just a question of taking more dope or drinking more wine, though admittedly that helps. I cheer myself up by writing novels where the human race gets into fatal trouble.

Personally, I am sweet-natured. Many women love me, as I love many women. My table manners are good. And I am cheerful despite what I have said above. But if I really want to cheer myself up greatly and have a laugh, I think of the funniest, bitterest joke I ever heard—told to me by a Russian Jewish friend.

The joke goes like this. (Historically, it comes from the time when Poland was under Soviet domination.

Polish jokes often take the form of riddles, as does this joke.)

Question: What stands on the corner of the street and does not kick people?

Answer: A Russian-made people-kicker.

If you can't laugh at that, you don't deserve to be happy!

Brian W. Aldiss is the author of many works of fiction, nonfiction, and poetry. He is most known for his celebrated works of science fiction, which have won several awards, including multiple Hugos and Nebulas. In 2005, Aldiss was awarded the title of Officer of the Order of the British Empire for services to literature.

Max Alexander

I'm a comic. A once-in-a-blue-moon actor. A foodaholic. I've a brother who killed two people. Am fifty-three and still single. I'm not only down in the dumps, I got a condo on the beach with a panoramic view of the "dumps." My name is actually on the rotary sign as you enter Dumpsville, right across the street from Our Lady of "What the Hell Did I Do to Deserve This Crap" High School.

Don't get me wrong. I'm not making excuses. Just drawing a picture. Having some real drama in my life, I'm just glad to have my health; some work (which I love to do); cash in my pocket; a great, great—did I say great?—brother (the rabbi, not the murderer, long story), Moshe, and his family; and last, but not least, a great friend and mentor, Jerry Lewis.

So what do I do when attacked by the dumps? Which either I could see coming or, with a blink of an eye, they could be waiting for me in my foyer. I really don't have a foyer, but I love saying the word *foyer*.

Well, a few things. First and foremost is food. Food

glorious food. Oh, how carbohydrates taste on the tongue and make the soul dance. Pizza! The prescription to the cure of a blue mood. Unfortunately, being a native New Yorker and living in Los Angeles (the capital of "Hey, it's just like New York pizza"), I have to settle for mediocrity. Every kosher deli in L.A. is a misnomer, and I don't even know what *misnomer* means . . . but it sounds right. There was a deli that had the "square" potato knish (potato pie, for the Episcopalians out there) shipped in from New York. They steamed it! Why don't you just defile a synagogue while you're at it?

Anyway, food is only a temporary solution. You eat, you get fat, and you're blue again!

But—and I know you never start a sentence with the word *but*, but screw the rules; I'm out of school—there are three things that always get me out of the blues:

1. Doing a good thing for someone.

It could be a stranger. It could be a friend. It could be big or it could be small. I won't tell you about the charitable things I do. If I tell you, it takes away the good feelings I achieve from doing them. I also know that when I get that uplifting feeling from doing charitable work, it won't make me fat!

2. Calling my brother Moshe.

We are three brothers. The oldest . . . a murderer by trade. Myself, a comic (having a brother that's a convicted killer takes the heat off me being a comic), and my Moshe, the rabbi. Even when there is no answer to my bluish feelings, I know there is someone out there who cares for me and feels my pain.

3. Going to someone who always sets me straight: Jerry Lewis.

Now, I know this won't help you as a reader, so I'm not going to bloviate on how I know this dear friend of mine. Maybe you'll see it on E! when I die (forty or fifty times during the sweeps). Just let me say this: This mentor has a way of seeing the light and, most important, the directions to get out of the little hamlet I like to call "Dumpsville."

Max Alexander is a comedian and actor. He has appeared several times on *The Tonight Show* and has acted in films such as *Punchline* with Tom Hanks and *Roxanne* starring Steve Martin. Alexander has also opened for many big names in Las Vegas, including Tom Jones and Frank Sinatra.

Richard Anderson

The world is imperfect. Be cognitive. Work hard. Stay out of politics.

Richard Anderson is a film and television actor who has appeared in more than forty films, including Stanley Kubrick's *Paths of Glory* and the critically acclaimed Charles Burnett film *The Glass Shield*. Anderson is also known for becoming the first actor to play the same role in two separate series, Oscar Goldman in both *The Six Million Dollar Man* and *The Bionic Woman*.

Richard Ayers

A few years ago I needed a lift. My life had changed. From 1947, I had been a freelance illustrator of comic book adventure stories; in 1986, when assignments had slacked off, I decided to "retire." Being a frugal couple, my wife and I managed comfortably, although I found reading books in the winters and loafing at the beach in the summers left me feeling I was missing something. I was asked by a magazine to write about my years illustrating comic book stories. My editor stressed he wanted me to write about how badly I was treated, but I wouldn't write anything negative about the editors or publishers I had worked for and still hoped to work with again.

The idea of writing a memoir about my years in comics inspired me to start typing. I got an outline finished and felt something was missing. . . . I didn't get the exciting feeling I had when illustrating. My wife, Lindy, suggested I missed drawing pictures. She was right! Writing words was boring to me. I needed to illustrate the words. Lindy agreed and told me to write and illustrate my autobiography as a comic book story! I felt excitement setting up my studio to start work on the autobiography while adding whimsy and humor to my stories. As I progressed, I showed my autobio to editors and friends, receiving favorable reactions.

Once I had forty pages done, a publisher said he wanted to publish the autobiography. We signed a contract and I finished three-hundred-plus pages—enough to publish my work in three paperback volumes, which we did, and to set out to publish those in one hardcover book. Alas, the press run for the three paperbacks was just over fifteen hundred. I ended up with no big profit from my autobio. I just have a small inventory left for requests for copies.

And now I am seeking a new publisher.

I have no "down-in-the-dumps" feeling, for I look to the future with a hundred-plus-page graphic novel also completed.

Illustrating comic book stories was my solution to correcting my downtime, and that was thanks to my wife encouraging me. Thanks, Lindy. Your love is very sustaining.

Richard Ayers is a cartoonist who is known for his artwork in many titles, including *Ghost Rider, The Incredible Hulk,* and *The Fantastic Four.* Ayers is famous for his work during the comic gold and silver ages, most notably for Marvel Comics and The Timely/Atlas/Marvel Group.

B

Babette E. Babich

I find that animals can almost always bring me joy. This is true when I am in my finest form and this is true especially when I am lost in sadness, down, desolate. My cats—indeed, any cat!—can do this, by dint of sheer beauty: their way of being in the world, their elegance. Even the clumsiest among them enjoys an impossible grace. But it may be that what delights me above all is the chance to touch them. To pet a cat, it has been said, is the privilege of stroking a tiger (a viewpoint most cats take without needing to be told . . .). Petting a purring cat, as the ever-helpful researchers of health and well-being have found, measurably reduces blood pressure. This calming reduction in blood pressure is apparently mutually beneficial.

Of course, if I am really down, disconsolate, a walk in a park or garden does literal wonders. It doesn't have to be New York City's Central Park or the Brooklyn Botanical Gardens or Fort Tryon Park, near Manhattan's Cloisters; it can be any city, any park, any country walk. And it doesn't have to be walking; it can be in-line skating along the Hudson or in the park (I don't have a bike and I don't do the city cross-country-ski thing, but I am sure that this would work, too), just as long as one can move with ease. For me, it's not about the exercise (just)—and that is why I left running off the list (which seems to me a kind of second job for those who engage in it). Instead, it is about the trees and the plants and the light of the sky, in every season. These are small things.

Walking in the natural world is all about the chance to notice small things. For me and for my spirit, just the sight of a squirrel, red or gray, or, as one sometimes sees them in New York, black, can do marvels: watching them hunt for nuts, even better; watching them bury acorns, digging a hole for the acorn and then delicately patting it down, using their front paws like careful little hands; watching them climb and descend trees in circular motion, chasing one another (whether in fury or in the hope of love); or seeing them suspend themselves like overfurred bats from tree trunks and branches. But, above all, watching them running, bounding sinuously as they go, furry body followed by an echoing tail—little knots of intention, of purposeful being, as the poet says, natural Prozac and chamomile for the soul! As a kind of payback for this delight, I try to walk around with shelled nuts in a little zip-lock bag most of the fall and winter. These, this is my idea, are *fancy* nuts: pecans and walnuts and almonds (I have found that cashews perplex them), the sort of nuts a city squirrel has likely never encountered in its life (except, of course, as handouts from New Yorkers like myself, who worry that giving peanuts salted in the shell to squirrels cannot be good for them . . .). Intriguingly, squirrels, the ones with good experiences, know my intentions and add to my joy by meeting me halfway: a little dance of giver and giftee. I give them the nuts shelled—to save them work, so I pretend. In truth, I am hoping to get them to eat the nut so that I can watch them (and they don't always do this). Because I like pecans, I tend to carry these preferentially and thus I have a snack on hand for myself. And that, too, is a cheering thing.

I began by mentioning cats and walks and blading, and ended with squirrels, just because I have found that afterward I can turn to friends and family. And yet I almost never turn to my friends or my family to cheer me up to begin with, firstly because that seems a touch unfair and secondly, maybe more crucially, so experience tells me, they, less keen on the wonders of squirrels than I am, may well be in need of someone to cheer them up themselves!

Babette E. Babich is a professor of philosophy at Fordham University as well as an adjunct research professor at Georgetown University. She is the author of several books and is the executive editor of *New Nietzsche Studies,* the journal of the Nietzsche Society. Babich recently received a Fulbright scholarship for her research on the philosophers Friedrich Nietzsche and Martin Heidegger and the poet Friedrich Hölderlin.

Burt Bacharach

For me, it's always helpful to connect with music, either listening or, much more preferable, playing and writing. I feel very blessed that I can make a living doing it. Sometimes, it's not writing at all that inspires me but playing at the piano, improvising and making contact with music. And then doing concerts and making people feel good absolutely makes me feel good and lifts me up in turn. Meditation is also a big plus.

Burt Bacharach is a Grammy- and Academy Award–winning composer and musician. He has written hit songs for many artists, including several for Dionne Warwick and Dusty Springfield. Bacharach has also written sound tracks for several films, such as *Butch Cassidy and the Sundance Kid* and the 1967 film *Casino Royale.* His songs continue to be popular among contemporary musicians of all genres.

Bob Balaban

Whenever I'm in a bad mood, which, fortunately, isn't all that often, I put my "feel better quick" scheme into action. Having acquired more than the cursory acquaintance with both group and individual therapy, as well as the collected works of Scott Peck and Dr. Phil, I have devised a simple, inexpensive solution to fighting the blues: I clean my room. I don't mean metaphorically. I mean literally.

I start by removing all the piles from my desk and dividing the whole mess into three stacks, labeled Keep, Store, and Throw Away. I discovered this technique in an article in the *Daily News* several years ago and found that it can take the edge off a mood swing quicker than a hot fudge sundae. If I'm still in trouble, I'll do drawers. I take everything out, strew the contents on my now clean desk, then go to Staples and buy a stack of colorful folders. I file my drawer contents into the folders, then put the folders into wire baskets, stack them next to my shoes, and forget about them.

If that doesn't work, it's on to my closet. First I remove the tangle of shirts that have been hurled three deep onto sagging wire hangers and give each one its own matching, brand-new wooden hanger. Another unexpected blues buster. It's also a golden opportunity to get rid of frayed or otherwise hopeless shirts I've been saving to wear when I garden, an activity in which I almost never engage.

As a very last-ditch resort I have been known to attack the stacks of paperwork that I hide behind the drapes, next to my air conditioner. Unfortunately, that stack usually contains stuff that I actually have to deal with, hence the "very."

I'm not sure why any of this works, but it does. For one thing, making order out of chaos can provide a reassuring feeling of being in control. Unfortunately, the only thing you are controlling is socks and paper clips. For another, shuffling around a bunch of inanimate objects for a sustained period of time can be pretty relaxing and may even be meditative. It's certainly mind-numbing. And a lot less dangerous than drugs. And much cheaper.

If none of the above makes you any happier, at least you will have an easier time locating your stuff, which, in the long run, may be even more important than happiness.

Bob Balaban is an actor and author. He has acted in several major motion pictures, including *Catch-22* and the Steven

Spielberg film *Close Encounters of the Third Kind*. Balaban is also known for his roles in the Christopher Guest films *Waiting for Guffman*, *Best in Show*, *A Mighty Wind*, and *For Your Consideration*. Balaban is currently writing a series of children's books about the adventures of a dog named McGrowl.

Kaye Ballard

When I need a little lift, I eat a huge bowl of pasta and I go out to a good movie (if I can find one).

Simple things in life make me happy! Shallow me.

Kaye Ballard is an accomplished singer and actress. She has performed in numerous prestigious nightclubs and has made television appearances on talk shows such as *The Tonight Show* and *The Carol Burnett Show*. Ballard has acted in several films, including *Freaky Friday* with Jodie Foster, and performed in various stage productions, such as *Gypsy, Funny Girl,* and *Follies.*

Taina Bien-Aimé

In my work at Equality Now, whose mission is to end violence and discrimination against women and girls around the world, I learn every day about atrocities perpetrated against the majority of the planet simply because it was born female: rape, domestic violence, female genital mutilation, honor killings, trafficking, acid burnings, and the list goes on without mercy. Every day, we tackle these issues by raising awareness, mobilizing public pressure to take action against these violations, and urging governments to abide by the laws they have signed to protect all of their citizens, regardless of gender. On days when victory seems too distant to bear, when political setbacks thwart our goals and fundraising hits every brick wall on the horizon, I admire Sisyphus. At least he was able to roll that rock up a few feet before he got knocked backed down that mountain. So when my head is about to burst and my heart sink, I crave a little lift. I head over to the closest playground, where my sons no longer tread. There, on sunny days, I stay until my lips curl into an irrepressible smile. I observe toddlerdom, a universe where walking babies reign with determination, terror, and fat bellies. At any moment, a diapered onlooker will yank a pacifier out of an unassuming mouth and either taste it himself or grind it into the sandbox to the horror of his playmate. A few feet away, pudgy feet run a sprinter's dash toward the gate, gleefully ignoring the loud pleas of an aggravated parent to please stop. By a tree, a curious pint-sized wanderer darts sticky fingers into a placid dog's nostrils or expresses shock and dismay when chased pigeons fly. I laugh, watching the alpha babies pull hair to get ahead on the slide or engage in tugs-of-war with plastic water buckets. The caregivers attempt to negotiate or cajole for a truce or just simply remove these feisty moppets into zones of temporary peace or to a stroller with an escape-proof harness. Above the cries desperate for naps or the tantrums that are intricate parts of the day's agenda, I take in the joy and love, which the world's children need more than air. These gleeful moments of discovery and wonder give me comfort and faith in the human race, whose failings can have such a cruel impact on the planet and on others. Right now, though, setting aside those details and relieved those diaper days have passed, I leave the park, my soul rejuvenated and thankful for humankind's gift to melt away despair and to unearth hope wherever we stand, even for a moment.

Taina Bien-Aimé is a former international lawyer who holds a Juris Doctor from the New York University School of Law and a License in Political Science from the University of Geneva and the Graduate School of International Studies in Switzerland. She is currently the executive director of Equality Now, an international human rights organization that works to end violence and discrimination against women and girls around the world.

Bill Boggs

First thing when I have descended into a bad mood is that I try to figure out why I have lost my normal buoyancy and optimism; I know there is a direct cause and effect for me—I don't fall into weird, unexplained bad moods by accident. So, I try to come to some conclusion about what's happened to me. I'm either hungry, mad at something or somebody, racing against time, pissed off at people honking horns excessively on the street below, annoyed at solicitation calls, overwhelmed with annoying details to attend to, whatever. I find some reason, so I don't feel I'm a loose-cannon psycho who's flipped to black and white from color without a button being pushed.

That little bit of knowledge helps, but then I have to do something to blast away the actual glumness, and nothing works better for me than a trip to the steam room and a thirty-minute swim in the pool at my athletic club. When I step out of the pool, I've transformed myself from being in a bad mood to being someone whose spirit more closely resembles that of nude people dancing around in the mud at Woodstock.

Bill Boggs is a four-time Emmy Award—winning television host and personality. He is the host of various television shows, including *Midday Live with Bill Boggs* and the Food Network hit *Bill Boggs Corner Table*. Boggs has pioneered numerous shows on Food Network and has interviewed celebrities for multiple television programs. Boggs was instrumental in the creation of the television network Court TV and is a featured columnist for several magazines.

Pat Boone

Who doesn't need a lift from time to time, an emotional or spiritual "goose" to get you back on stride? I sure do.

I read the Bible through from cover to cover every year; I'm not saying that to sound pious. In fact, it's because I know my weaknesses, my humanity, my failings—and I get slapped around by life and its disappointments like anybody else.

That's one of the great things about the Bible; it lets you know that virtually everybody in there has been subject to the same knockdowns and failures we all experience. The disappointments crush some, but others, the ones that inspire us, find the answers—and that's what I look for.

King David is described as "a man after God's own heart." Pretty good, huh? To have God Himself describe you that way? Well sure, but David made some grievous mistakes, for which he paid dearly; he had many enemies and a turbulent life. His own son Absalom rebelled against him, tried to take his kingdom from him, and was willing to kill his own father.

Listen to this, from Psalm 41, David's own words:

All who hate me whisper together against me;
Against me they devise my hurt.
"An evil disease," they say, "clings to him.
And now that he lies down, he will rise up no more."
Even my own familiar friend in whom I trusted,
Who ate my bread,
Has lifted up his heel against me.

He continues, in his deep funk, in the 42nd Psalm:

Why are you cast down, O my soul?
And why are you disquieted within me?
Hope in God:
For I shall yet praise Him,
The help of my countenance and my God.

In the *Living Bible* translations of that passage, which I love, he says, "O my soul, why be so gloomy and discouraged? Trust in God! I shall again praise Him for his wondrous help to me; He will make me smile again *For He is my God!"*

Let's face it: Life is a school, from beginning to end. How did you learn whatever math you studied at school? By memorizing rules and formulas? Oh, you probably did that, but then you were given *problems,* so that you could put those principles to work. And if you did, you got the correct answers, right?

So when I get down and discouraged, and really need a lift, I follow the example of King David. I think back over all the ways and times God has blessed me and brought me through other knotholes and difficulties, and I realize He'll bring me through the current ones as well. I preach to my own soul, like David did, and I literally talk to my friend, my God, in gratitude and praise.

He's never left me in the dumps yet.

Pat Boone is a recording artist, actor, author, and American icon. With thirty-eight Top 40 hits and more than 45 million units sold, Boone is *Billboard* magazine's #10 rock recording artist in history. He has also acted in several films, including *Journey to the Center of the Earth* and *The Greatest Story Ever Told*. His book *'Twixt Twelve and Twenty* was a #1 best-seller for two years. In 2003, Boone was inducted into the Gospel Music Hall of Fame for his hit song "Under God."

Bobby Bowden

When I am down in the dumps, which is seldom, I want only to be with my wife, Ann. I don't want to have anyone else around. I prefer to get out of town and go to our condominium in Panama City, which is on the fourteenth floor of a high-rise.

During this time and in this setting, I feel secure and away from the vise that is choking me. It gives me a chance to talk to Ann and find a solution to whatever is bothering me. Also, I get free from my depression by reading some of my favorite military books about my war heroes, including Generals Patton, MacArthur, Napoleon, Rommel, Bradley, Montgomery, Lee, Jackson, Grant . . . etc. I'll read and get lost in the great battles these men fought.

Soon I will recall that they all had problems like I do and as all public figures do. I will then have a Bible study and prayer with Ann, and by that time I realize I'm the luckiest guy in the world! "Dumps" are defeated!

Bobby Bowden is a coach of NCAA Division 1A football. Bowden holds the most career wins in Division 1A football history and is currently the head coach for Florida State University, where he has been since 1976. In 2004, the Fellowship of Christian Athletes created a yearly award in Bowden's name, and a bronze statue of Bowden stands in front of Doak Campbell Stadium at Florida State.

Donna L. Brazile

When I need a little lift from all the day's drama, all the political brushfires I must put out or the Katrina fatigue I have experienced from the past year, I take out my cast-iron pot. Yes, I find my joy in cooking up something spicy and delicious. No matter if I am happy or sad, it lifts me up.

One of my favorite items to cook is popcorn. You see, my parents did not have a lot of money, but they found creative ways to reward their nine kids for good behavior. Once a month, my dad, Lionel, who got paid on the twenty-fifth, would go out and purchase a gallon jug of vanilla ice cream and gingerbread cookies. The rest of the month, we made popcorn.

My mother, Jean, did not like us messing around in the kitchen. But after dinner, she would allow me to come in and use her cast-iron skillet to prepare the popcorn. This was a delicious treat.

Now I still enjoy coming home and preparing delicious Cajun and Creole meals like shrimp étouffée or crayfish jambalaya. All these dishes are made to my mother's perfection. But when I am in that particular mood, feeling like the world is crashing all around me, I like to make a simple bowl of popcorn.

Here's what I do: Pull out Mama Jean's old black skillet. Pour some grease (forget the olive oil) and add a little dash of salt. Now let it get good and hot and stir in some yellow popcorn. As the kernels heat up, I look down and smell the wonderful aroma. By the time the skillet is good and hot, I place the lid and start to twist and shout. Yep, it is called the popcorn dance and I find it the best way to cure the blues, get rid of my funk, and overcome any negative thoughts.

When I am done stirring all those nasty bad vibes out of my system, I open the lid, smell the popcorn, season it well, and then pour it in my big white popcorn bowl. I take it upstairs and my little Pomeranian, Chip, and I sit in front of the TV smiling from cheek to cheek.

Donna L. Brazile is the founder and managing director of Brazile and Associates, LLC; chair of the Democratic National Committee's Voting Rights Institute (VRI); and an adjunct professor at Georgetown University. Brazile was included in *Washingtonian Magazine*'s 100 Most Powerful Women in Washington, D.C., and received the Congressional Black Caucus Foundation's Award for Political Achievement. She is the author of *Cooking With Grease,* a memoir about her life and work in politics.

David Brenner

When I was fourteen years old, I operated rides at the Woodside Amusement Park in my hometown of Philadelphia. The hours were 9:00 a.m. to closing time, which depended on the weather and how many customers were in the park, so sometimes I left as early as 9:00 p.m., but most often I worked until about 2:00 a.m., a good seventeen-hour day, seven days a week, for a total of 119 hours a week. This doesn't include the two hours it took by bus and subway to get to and from work, which left me a daily three hours to brush my teeth, go to the bathroom, and sleep. It's so much fun to be poor.

After punching out, it was about a three-city-block walk through the dark park to the bus stop, where I would catch the first of two buses, the second of which would drop me off at the elevated train that would take me to a five-block walk to my row house. The only other building in this area of the park was an insane asylum that was behind tall, thick stone walls. Not the most pleasant spot to wait for a bus late at night, but there was no choice.

One chilly September night it started to rain hard, a city monsoon, so the park closed around 11:00 p.m. That's the good news. The bad news is that after the long walk to the bus stop, there was no protection under which to stand. The buses ran every forty-five minutes and I had seen the rear lights of one when I was about two blocks away, so I had a full wait.

As the temperature dropped, the rain become harder, until it was a torrential downpour in the cold of the night. I was a tall kid, 6 foot 2 and skinny, weighing 145 pounds. Cold always ripped through me to the bones. In minutes, I was shivering, which soon turned to uncontrollable shaking.

I started lamenting about being poor, which had forced me to start working more than thirty hours a week before my ninth birthday and never allowed me to have the proper clothing for any of the four seasons. Lamenting turned into anger and feeling sorry for me and hating the world and swearing aloud about being somebody someday and never being cold, wet, and hungry ever again . . . everything I always thought about and felt, when life was doing the slapping and I was doing the receiving.

At my lowest moment, I had an epiphany. It was as if someone or something took random words I had spoken in my life, scrambled them into another order, and slipped them into my mind.

"David, do you know how many dead people would trade places with you right now?"

It almost bowled me over. I thought of people rotting in coffins being pounded by this rain and how they would love to be fourteen years old, alive, standing wet and cold, waiting for a bus to arrive to begin the trip to a warm home in which there were sleeping two marvelous parents, a sister, and a brother. A poor but safe, loving haven.

The bus finally came; the next bus arrived after about a fifteen-minute wait in the doorway of a bar; then came the elevated train, the walk through the drenched streets, a stoop taken two steps at a time, the creaking wooden slats of the porch, the cold brass doorknob, and the comforting warmth of home and love.

From that teenage night to this very moment, whenever life attacks rather than caresses, when I start to slip into a pool of negative thoughts and a bad mood, I think about all the dead people who would trade places with me, and I continue to survive.

David Brenner is a writer, producer, and comedian. Known for his stand-up comedy, Brenner has been a regular on *The Tonight Show* and *David Letterman*. According to the *Book of Lists #2,* Brenner has been the most frequent talk show guest among all entertainers. He has also had four HBO specials, which rank among some of HBO's highest rated. Before becoming a comic, Brenner enjoyed a successful career in documentary filmmaking that earned him nearly thirty awards, including an Emmy.

Beau Bridges

When I need a little lift, I think of all the blessings in my life. This usually changes my perspective and helps me get to a more positive place.

Beau Bridges is an American actor. He is best known for his role of Major General Hank Landry on the popular television series *Stargate SG-1.* He played the same character in some of the episodes of the spin-off series, *Stargate Atlantis.* Bridges has also guest-starred on hit television series such as *Will and Grace* and *My Name Is Earl.*

Bernie Brillstein

Unfortunately, when I'm in a bad mood, the first thing I think of is food. Most often it's simple food. It could be a Danish pastry or it could be a piece of coffee cake. But when I'm really feeling down, I think of a tuna fish sandwich on white toast with a Diet Coke and a slice of lemon.

As I sit alone in my kitchen, I turn on ESPN, eat my sandwich, drink my Diet Coke, and remember that my beautiful house is all paid for. My wife is asleep with Lucy, our dog, lying next to her and I luxuriate in the fact that when you come down to it, life is really as simple as a good tuna fish sandwich on white toast.

P.S.: I have no idea why it's tuna fish but I'm sure it goes back to my childhood.

Bernie Brillstein is a top packager and producer, personal manager, and consultant in the entertainment industry. Brillstein has shaped the careers of numerous stars, including Dan Aykroyd, Brad Pitt, Nicolas Cage, and several former

Saturday Night Live cast members. He has helped produce several hit television shows and films, including the Oscar-winning film *Dangerous Liaisons.* Brillstein is a cofounder of Brillstein-Grey Entertainment, one of Hollywood's premier talent agencies.

Erin Brockovich

The very moment that I feel down, depressed, or full of despair, I immediately hear my mother's voice: "Erin, when the going gets tough, the tough get going." "Pick yourself up by your bootstraps and keep on moving." "Never let the bastards get you down." And then she would remind me of the power of a little-known word: *stick-to-itiveness.* Definition: the propensity to follow through in a determined manner. Dogged persistence born out of obligation and stubbornness.

Whenever I call upon my mother's voice and I hear that word, *stick-to-itiveness,* I begin to visualize the little engine that could. I think I can, I know I can, and by God, I *do*!

Whenever I go down, and believe me, I do, I allow myself a short and brief pity party, which is always quite fun. I give myself the time to lie on the couch, cry, eat potato chips, and watch *Oprah* all day long, and then enough is enough and I get up and spring into action.

I find the soothing voice and words of wisdom of my mother to be better than a box of chocolate, a bottle of booze, or a "nooner." The "little engine that could" must have believed in stick-to-itiveness, which can always turn a bad day into one of hope and inspiration.

There is always another day and another moment, so don't let it get you down, at least not for long.

Erin Brockovich is a former legal clerk who helped to spearhead the largest direct-action lawsuit of its kind against the Pacific Gas and Electric Company. The suit won the largest toxic injury settlement in U.S. history, totaling $333 million in damages. An Academy Award–winning film starring Julia Roberts was made about the story. Today Brockovich is a public speaker highly in demand and president of the consulting firm Brockovich Research & Consulting.

Danielle Broussard

I am a big believer in the idea that there is very little that a new pair of shoes and a Klondike bar can't fix. A Dove Bar, if it's really bad. But sometimes blatant self-indulgence is just not enough. I admit that I am one of those ridiculously sensitive types who can be thrown into a bad mood because someone in line at the post office sighed when I asked the clerk if there was another choice of stamp, holding things up another ten seconds. I will stay in a foul funk until I see something like two New Yorkers with different native tongues attempting to curse each other out in English. "I am yelling f*ck at you, my friend!" Laughing at anything stupid that humans do, or sincerely sweet a child does, can usually revive me. I experience enough bad moments to need sugar administered at least twice daily. I also have the habit of crying at least once a day. Anything can trigger this. I stopped watching *Biography* for this very reason. They make you fall in love with the person and then BAM! they *always* die at the end. I didn't know that daily tear duct cleansing was unusual until my husband told me. Actually, I asked him, "You mean every-body else doesn't?" Who knew? All this swinging from happy to sad in an instant makes some think of manic de-pression. I prefer to call it living in the moment.

There was one time, though, where I was too far down for a good laugh or red velvet cake to pull me out. After a year of declining health, two operations, chronic pain, fa-tigue, and no answers, I decided to try something out of desperation that could potentially be more painful than ac-cepting the hand I'd been dealt. I decided to find my birth mother so I could ask about my biological family's medical history. In short, she not only wouldn't give me access to my own health history, she denied my own existence . . . to me.

It is hard to find your self-worth when the very first thing that happened to you was being discarded like trash. Logically, I know this says more about her than me. But there is a part of your soul that is forever bruised with the query, If my own mother couldn't love me, who can? You walk through your life waiting for the next person to reject you. Why *would* they want me? She didn't. What makes me worthy now? No orphan believes that just being born is enough reason to be loved, because you know what? It wasn't. No single episode has given me more doubts about humanity. If she could do this, again, why *wouldn't* perfect strangers hurt each other?

The darkness descended upon me until I could no longer discuss it with my husband. I couldn't understand her actions and my husband couldn't understand why I didn't just reject her back and be done with it. There will be no answers. Move on. I took to crying in the living room out of earshot. As I was lying prostrate on my couch, crying my eyes out for the umpteenth time, something happened. At my darkest hour, one I didn't want another human being to see, my cat jumped up and nestled in the crack of my ass. And I laughed. Divine intervention or random search for warmth? Not sure. It doesn't matter. Because it brought me back from a place that no child or adult should ever be, and reminded me that there is such a thing as unconditional love. Hell, my cat loves me so much she needs to be sedated when I go on road gigs!

My severed roots don't matter as much as whom I love and let love me now; I was asking the wrong question all along. It's not, Can anyone love me? It's, Can I love unconditionally? And that answer is, Yes.

Every time I open the door and see my cats, I realize I love them just because they're there. I don't need another reason. Being born is reason enough. That's love. So whenever I'm sad, I just kiss my cats, and hope that I love them well enough that they don't miss their birth mother too much.

Danielle Broussard has been a stand-up comic for over ten years. She is a regular at the Comic Strip Live and the Comedy Cellar in New York City. She has also appeared on *Late Night with Conan O'Brien* and was a semifinalist on the television show *Last Comic Standing.* She has recently provided comedy commentary for various television shows on *VH1.*

Dave Brubeck

If I am feeling blue, I listen to my favorite jazz recordings by Louis Armstrong or Erroll Garner. They never fail to make me smile.

Dave Brubeck is one of the most well-known jazz pianists of all time. The Dave Brubeck Quartet, which lasted for seventeen years, was responsible for the first-ever jazz song to sell more than a million copies. Brubeck continues to tour and release albums and was the inspiration for the Brubeck Institute at the University of the Pacific, his alma mater. The institute promotes not only jazz studies but also social and philosophical issues.

Carol Burnett

Before you go to bed, write down three "gratefuls" for the day and three "did wells" (they can even include something as simple as doing the laundry)—the results can be amazing!

Carol Burnett is an American comedian most famous for the popular *Carol Burnett Show,* which ran for eleven years and won twenty-two Emmy Awards. Before her hit variety show, Burnett acted on Broadway in productions such as *Once Upon a Mattress.* She also had success on *The Garry Moore Show,* where she won an Emmy. Recently, Burnett has appeared on the hit television program *Desperate Housewives* and in 2003 was the recipient of the Kennedy Center Honors.

Barbara Bush

I cheer up when I reread a Jane Austen book or watch any of the Austen films on the BBC. I find these amusing and it makes me happy. I own all of her works on tape, film, and in book form. Any of Austen's beautiful works of art allows me to take my mind off of politics and make me ready to face life's problems.

Barabara Bush is a former first lady to President George H. W. Bush and the mother of President George W. Bush. While serving as first lady, she championed literacy as her special cause, becoming the honorary chairman of the Barbara Bush Foundation for Family Literacy. Today, Bush serves on the boards of AmeriCares and the Mayo Clinic and continues her prominent role in the Barbara Bush Foundation.

Gov. Jeb Bush

I firmly believe we all need to love living and life more, so we don't get down in the dumps. We need to be more willing to turn adversity and unhappiness into something positive. Dealing with bad stuff isn't always fun, but if you get beyond thinking about always having fun, and look at the joy in solving a problem, developing a solution, or overcoming an obstacle, the personal satisfaction of being able to say "I did it!" will make you feel great.

Prevention is the key to avoiding being in the dumps, but occasionally we all fall prey to it. I find a round or two of speed golf helps clear my head. If that doesn't work, getting a deep body massage usually does the trick. . . . There's nothing like having someone stick their elbow into your spine to make you feel better!

Gov. Jeb Bush has served as the governor of the state of Florida for two terms. During this time Bush has revolutionized Florida's education system and sought to strengthen and diversify Florida's economy and protect its natural environment. Before becoming a governor, Bush served as Florida's secretary of commerce. He is the son of President George H. W. Bush and Barbara Bush and the brother of President George W. Bush.

C

Grethe Cammermeyer

Being asked to write how you deal with being down is challenging. At first I went through denial. I am never in the dumps. Then the reality hit me of how I felt really overwhelmed by emotional pain when I did not get custody of the kids during a predivorce separation, and later when I lost my commission as a military officer because of my statement that I was a lesbian.

The pain associated with those losses was so overwhelming that I would be much more than "down in the dumps." I certainly contemplated suicide, not sure that I would survive. I felt like my heart was being crushed and I could not catch my breath. How to go on? Even writing about those experiences is like reliving them all over again, even though they took place years ago.

Emotional survival comes with surviving the experience. First you breathe, still emotionally unsure of how you will survive. There was such an enormous sense of loss of something familiar—kids, family, and a military career—that was part of a personal identity.

After knowing I was not going to die from the emotional pain, I had to learn how to live as a different person and have a different image of myself. It is quite amazing how society helps you form a mental picture of who you are and how you play into that role. Being a divorcée whose children were with their father was a taboo at the time. Being gay and in the military was an oxymoron from society's understanding of homosexuality. I had internalized negative perceptions about myself, which made moving forward, and creating a new life as a whole person, difficult.

My personal makeup and spiritual belief is that everything happens for a purpose. Although finding the purpose can be elusive, I began looking for a meaning.

Fortunately, I was a very good nurse, motivated and always looking for the best way to care for my patients, which was my driving force for pursuing a PhD in nursing science. Looking for meaning in loss gave me the professional opportunity to "be all that I could be" as a nurse. And I came to be recognized by both the military and the VA for my clinical expertise.

Curiously, over time, that professional development also helped me spiritually to feel that I was whole, not fragmented as I had felt earlier in my life. In becoming more grounded I also became a better mother and now a grandmother. And being whole also enabled me to develop a real, emotional bonding with my life partner of eighteen years.

It is my life experience that has given me the passion to continue to speak out on behalf of gays and lesbians who serve in the military today but who have to do so in silence. I do believe that the early funk, holding on to life by a thread, surviving and having an extraordinary life, requires that the meaning of my life is to speak out on behalf of those who cannot. We create our own meaning for our lives and in so doing, offer hope to others.

I know that if I am uncomfortable, it is where I need to be: to speak out, to challenge bias, to work for social justice.

Grethe Cammermeyer is a former military nurse who reached the rank of colonel and earned several awards. Cammermeyer was dismissed from the military when she revealed that she was a lesbian and took the matter to court. She was reinstated after she won her case. Cammermeyer wrote an award-winning autobiography titled *Serving in Silence,* which was later turned into an Emmy Award–winning made-for-television movie. Today she runs a radio talk show and focuses on her family.

Rhonda Fleming Carlson

At an early age I found refuge from the anxieties of life through my faith in God, which instilled in me an optimism and spirit of well-being that directed my path away from doubt and depression. Although I've had times when I've felt at odds with a particular situation, circumstance, or unforeseen tragedy I've encountered, I've always found solace in meditating quietly, taking a long walk, and observing God's amazing creations in the world, which also heightens my awareness of the many blessings in my life.

Rhonda Fleming Carlson is a successful actress, appearing in more than forty films, including *Spellbound* directed by Alfred Hitchcock. She has acted alongside stars such as Kirk Douglas, Charlton Heston, Rock Hudson, and Ronald Reagan. Carlson has also had a successful career on Broadway and has guest-starred on several major television shows. She is a founding member of Stop Cancer and works with numerous organizations to help abused and homeless children, among other causes.

Jackie Chan

Well, most of the time I am in a good mood, but sometimes even I have a bad day. The one thing that is guaranteed to put me into a good mood is a visit with my puppies, Jones and JJ. If I come home in a dark mood, my puppies will cheer me up—they are so excited to see me and are so adoring. I love watching them grow and teaching them and seeing them change from these wild little animals into ones that are disciplined and properly trained. They still have a lot to learn, but they are very eager and enthusiastic. Yes, my dogs always make me feel happy.

Another thing that nearly always puts me into a good mood is a vigorous workout. I will run on my treadmill, lift weights, and do some boxing. Exercising is good for health, and the chemicals that our bodies release during exercise are good for our emotions. During my workouts I find that I can think very clearly, and when I'm finished I always feel better mentally and physically.

Finally, I have to mention the feeling that I get from

doing charity work. Visiting the people who benefit from my charities and seeing their happy faces always makes me feel good. The absolute best is visiting with the children in remote areas of China and attending the opening of one of the schools that we've built through the charity. It's impossible not to smile when I see all the happy faces of the children. The people who benefit from the charities probably think that they're the ones who are happiest because of what they've been given. They won't ever know how deeply their joy affects me as well.

When I travel around for my charities, I always end up learning about new issues. I have two choices: I can avoid them or deal with them. I choose to deal with them. My choice to involve myself with helping others is very meaningful and always makes me happy. I think that people need to recognize how important a positive attitude is and how being optimistic can affect your life. If you always concentrate on the negative, you will be in a bad mood all the time and nothing—not even puppies or charity work—will make you happy.

Jackie Chan is an international film star best known for his martial arts skill. Films such as *Drunken Master, Rumble in the Bronx,* and the *Rush Hour* and *Shanghai Noon* series have secured Chan's position as one of the world's leading kung fu actors. Along with film, Chan takes his work as an ambassador for UNICEF/UNAIDS very seriously, and as stated above, devotes much time and effort to charity work.

Chubby Checker

I seek the truth. And every word that comes out of the mouth of God is that. It sets my mind at ease. It soothes me . . . until the Devil shows his ugly head again.

Chubby Checker is a Grammy Award—winning musician. Most famous among his long list of hits is "The Twist," which revolutionized dancing in the sixties and is the only single to reach #1 on the charts twice, once during its initial release and again upon its rerelease. Additionally, Checker is the only artist to have five albums in the Top 12 at the same time, as well as the only artist to have nine double-sided hits.

Walter Chwals, MD

When I am down, I think of how fortunate I am in so many ways. I think of the love and support of family, the warmth and fellowship of good friends; and sometimes just the thought of something as elegantly simple as the pure glee in an infant's smile or my sister's sublimely delicious Christmas candy will allow me to feel upbeat and let me concentrate on working to fix a problem or striving to make life better. I always try to remember that the situation can be worse and to count my blessings. I try to remember also that, through effort and goodwill, I can effect positive change and improve my life and, hopefully, the lives of others.

Walter Chwals, MD, is a pediatric trauma surgeon at the Rainbow Babies and Children's Hospital in Cleveland, Ohio. As well as being one of the country's top pediatric surgeons, Chwals is a professor at the Case Western Reserve University School of Medicine, where he teaches and conducts his own research. He has published articles in journals such as *The Journal of Pediatric Surgery and Pediatric Neurosurgery.*

Liz Claman

I could sit here and be all *Playboy* centerfold-ish and say, "I look at a child's smiling face to give me a pickup" or "I run a couple of miles and I *always* feel much better!" but the fact is, I've found a few little "recipes" that work so much better.

Setting out to find the perfect lipstick color eats up time and keeps you focused on something so banal that you can't help but forget your troubles. And once you do find it (which, by the way, you never will, especially if you're a redhead like me), you're only out about twenty bucks.

Then there's the call-up-a-sister-and-engage-in-catty-gossip strategy. I have three sisters, one of whom is always game for this activity. It always feels so nice to tear down other people in order to build oneself up, right? Keep in mind, the targets of the gossip must be other members of the family. That's the only way this one works.

Baking a pie and eating would work, but I find that takes way too long, especially when you're in desperate need of a mood improvement, so I prefer to indulge in the slice-and-bake cookies you get in the dairy section of any supermarket. They work just as well and if you're feeling really low, skip the baking step and eat the cookie dough raw.

Finally, if all else fails, rent *The Freshman* starring Marlon Brando and Matthew Broderick.

Liz Claman is an award-winning journalist and news anchor. She won an Emmy for her work at WEWS-TV (ABC) in Cleveland, as well as a local Emmy for KCBS-TV in Los Angeles. Claman is currently an anchor for CNBC and has worked on shows such as *Wake Up Call, Morning Call,* and *MarketWrap.* Her first book, *The Best Investment Advice I Ever Received,* was published in November 2006.

Denton A. Cooley, MD

Many of my great joys have occurred at the Texas Heart Institute, where I have spent my surgical career. And while infrequent, most of my disappointments have occurred there, too. When patients do not do well, my emotions are vulnerable. A change of scenery and atmosphere helps most, and golf usually seems to be the perfect solution. It rids me of some frustrations and gives me new ones! Moreover, I enjoy the exercise and the fellowship with golfers who are not involved in medicine but have their own worries in their professions.

Whether surgery or golf, at the end of each day, I determine to give it my best again tomorrow.

Denton A. Cooley, MD, is a world-renowned cardiovascular surgeon who has impressed surgeons around the world with his speed and dexterity in the operating room and his innovations in heart surgery. In 1967, Cooley was granted the prestigious René Leriche Prize by the International Surgical Society. Cooley founded the Texas Heart Institute in Houston, where he has performed as many as twenty-five heart operations in a single day.

Wes Craven

No pun intended, but when I need a lift I go to a hardware store.

Sounds funny, I know, but tools are wonderful things. And not just power tools, although a good bench saw can be downright magical. But pliers, wrenches, saws, planes—simple tools with few or no moving parts that do one specific thing really, really well—these are among the good things in life. To hold, say, a set of carbide-tipped brad-point drills nestled in their wooden box, that's a happy moment. Beautifully machined, elegantly simple, free of swooshes or bling. Things like that lift my spirit. They are mute testament to human ingenuity and remind me that craftsmanship still counts in this world.

Besides, it's great to buy something you know you can use the rest of your life, then pass on to your grandkids, and that when those kids are old, it'll still be doing its job well.

How many things are there like that left in life?

Maybe good movies.

Wes Craven is a screenwriter and director whose films are immensely popular. Craven is responsible for numerous blockbusters, including the classic *A Nightmare on Elm Street* and all three *Scream* films. He also directed the Oscar-nominated film *Music of the Heart* starring Meryl Streep. A 2006 remake of his second film, *The Hills Have Eyes,* has enjoyed box office success and a sequel has been released.

Mario Cuomo

If I find myself seriously beset by depressingly negative thoughts, or just by an old-fashioned funk, I do one of three things:

First, I try thinking about how people I know are in worse shape, or how I might be in worse shape. This is designed to make me feel, comparatively, less unhappy. If instead it makes me feel worse, then I try moving into what I call the State of Kinetic—going into constant motion . . . running, walking fast, rearranging books in my library, or my favorite, shining shoes, furiously . . . all the shoes in the house! Do you remember the old bromide "Idle hands are the Devil's workshop"? In the State of Kinetic, nothing is idle. By the time I've exhausted myself, I'm usually too tired to feel depressed . . . or anything else.

If neither of these things work, then, as the good nuns suggested, I just "offer up" my unhappiness as reparation for my sins. That doesn't necessarily make me happy either, but at least it allows me to think I just avoided a little bit of the really heavy punishment that comes after the ultimate accounting.

"Ultimate accounting"? WOW, now I *am* depressed!

Mario Cuomo was the governor of the state of New York from 1983 to 1995. He is known for his liberal political views, such as his opposition to the death penalty and his pro-choice stance on abortion, even though he is personally opposed to it. Cuomo is the author of two books, *Why Lincoln Matters: Today More Than Ever* and *Reason to Believe.* He is currently a lawyer at Willkie Farr & Gallagher LLP.

Jamie Lee Curtis

A Poem for Joy

When I'm blue
Or feeling sad
I think of things
That make me glad

My children will
Materialize
Their reminding not
To awfulize

The "first things first"
Old adage rule
Old-fashioned, yes
But useful tool

I think of things
Both don'ts and dos
I talk to friends
Avoid the news

A ball of sorts
I like to smash
I eat some chips
I read some trash

I wear things soft
And cozy warm
I hunker down
Ride out the storm

I make my lists
Of gratitude
I cry and moan
I sulk and brood

Watch MTV
And hoochie mas
Who all seem lost
Who wear no bras

I let my man
Make me some tea
I listen to
The "Blue" Joni

I drink fruit punch
Put on face cream
I try to sleep
Bring on a dream

And when I wake
I breathe and pray
The promise of
This brand-new day

I make contact
My girl and boy
And friends and fam
Who bring me JOY

I then go back
Into life's pond
And dance with wolves
And pass it on . . .

Jamie Lee Curtis is a world-famous actress and the author of several children's books. Curtis was initially nicknamed the "Scream Queen" due to her roles in horror films such as the *Halloween* movies, but she quickly proved that she could act in any genre, starring in films such as *A Fish Called Wanda, My Girl,* and *True Lies.* Her children's books are critically acclaimed and have spent numerous weeks on best-seller lists.

D

Charlie Daniels

I would be the first to admit that I may not be the most qualified person to participate in this project because I just don't spend a lot of time down in the dumps. I don't have time for it. I believe that being happy is a conscious decision and one that we have to make on a regular basis.

Are you going to look at setbacks as stumbling blocks or stepping stones? Are you going to let somebody else's evaluation of you affect the way you look at yourself? After all, don't you know what you're made out of more than they do? Sticks and stones . . .

Are you going to waste your time knocking the chip off someone's shoulder or taking offense at every little barb thrown your way? Or arguing with somebody about some point that in the scheme of things doesn't mean a doggone thing?

I love Jesus Christ and try to follow his teachings. I love my family and try to spend quality time with them. I love my country and try to serve it. I love my work and try to immerse myself in it.

Holding grudges pollutes the mind and unsettles the soul. I try to practice forgiveness in all things. It unloads the conscience and frees our mental processes to think about something constructive.

Letting go of the past is sometimes a struggle, but each day is a new opportunity. You can't do anything about what has happened, but you can sure do something about what is going to happen.

Idle hands and idle minds can drag you down. Stay busy, stay happy, and stay out of the dumps.

Charlie Daniels is an award-winning musician and, with the Charlie Daniels Band, has recorded multiple platinum albums. Daniels cowrote the song "It Hurts Me," sung by Elvis Presley and played on three Bob Dylan albums. His song "The Devil Went Down to Georgia" topped both the pop and the country charts, won a Grammy, and earned three Country Music Association trophies.

Tony Danza

My remedy is my ukulele. I sit and strum my blues away. My prescription: Get a uke and a chord book, practice thirty minutes a day for thirty days, and you will be able to entertain yourself, your family, and your friends for the rest of your life.

Tony Danza is an Emmy-nominated actor and former talk show host. Before becoming a television star, Danza was a professional boxer, but he left the trade when he landed a role in the sitcom *Taxi,* which ran for five years. He then went on to star in the sitcom *Who's the Boss?* Danza has also had a successful stage career, acting in *The Iceman Cometh* and *The Producers.*

Spencer Davis

As you may or may not know, I have been a professional musician for more than forty years. During this period, I have traveled all over the world and met people from all walks of life—ordinary people with ordinary jobs and people who have made fortunes. What I have found singularly interesting is that many people, from opposite ends of the financial spectrum, are very happy and content with their respective stations in life.

I started in music simply because I derived great pleasure from playing and, more important, from hearing other people playing. I never thought for one moment what was, and still is, my hobby would turn into my lifelong occupation and profession. When I have my moments of doubt and falter, I often think of the many people I have met on my forays into and around the world.

I remember some of the conversations after shows, when I heard how others dealt with their lows. I learned, and am still learning, from those strangers who populate our world how to live!

Spencer Davis is a musician who created the famed Spencer Davis Group and has recorded close to a dozen Top 10 hits. Tours with bands like the Rolling Stones and the Who and hit songs such as "Gimme Some Lovin'" won Davis great success in his native England and eventually throughout the world. Davis continues to tour and share his music with millions of fans worldwide.

Sugar Pie DeSanto

Whenever I'm feeling down or feel I'm at the end of my rope with daily stress, I go to my piano and write a song.

Sometimes it relates to things that have happened or things that are happening now. The music blocks out the problems and brings a new perspective to my life.

I've been an entertainer for more than fifty-five years. I look forward to continuing and perhaps bringing joy to others. My problems are small compared to some people's, so if I feel down, I sing a song or write one.

Sugar Pie DeSanto is one of the greatest female R&B and soul vocalists of her time. She was a regular at the Apollo Theater in New York and, after he saw her perform, became James Brown's opening act for two years. She has written more than a hundred songs, two of which she recorded as duos with Etta James. DeSanto is known for her powerful voice and show-stopping live performances.

Phyllis Diller

Happiness is a habit and I have cultivated it all my life. My life is about spreading cheer.

If I *ever* feel the slightest vague feeling of gloom, I get a joke book and read. In a matter of moments I am laughing out loud and feeling fine.

P.S.: My mantra is a daily upper.

My Mantra

On this happy day
I am thankful
For my blessings
And I pray
For renewed belief
In myself
And others
And hope
This bond of love
Will expand
To envelope
The entire universe.

Phyllis Diller is an iconic stand-up comic. She is known for her self-deprecating style of stand-up, as well as for her distinctive laugh. During the 1960s, Diller starred in many television specials with Bob Hope; she has recently lent her voice to the animated film *A Bug's Life* as well as several animated series. Diller has also recorded various comedy albums and is regarded as a pioneer of comedy.

Bob Dole

When I need a little lift . . . I think of all the positive things in my life. I think of the many challenges I've overcome to reach the present day. I think of the many great men and women of my generation—some of whom I knew and many others I didn't, some of whom lived to see this day and others who didn't—who served with me during World War II and in public life since. Then I think of the outstanding young people today who are as committed as we are to making a difference in the world and making this country what it should be.

Bob Dole is an American politician and decorated army veteran. Dole served as a Republican senator for his home state of Kansas from 1969 to 1996, during which time he served as both Senate minority and majority leader. He left this office to run for president in 1996, but lost to Democrat Bill Clinton. Dole continues to be a figure in American politics, writing books and appearing on television shows such as *The Daily Show* and *Larry King Live.*

Olympia Dukakis

When I am down, there are no dumps I've visited that I didn't like because I knew there was some insight to be had. Eleanor Roosevelt said, "Better to light a candle than to curse the dark." As wonderful as that seems, I prefer what Judy Grahn says: "Better to uncurse the dark."

Olympia Dukakis is a critically acclaimed actress. She has starred in films such as *Steel Magnolias, Mr. Holland's Opus,* and *Moonstruck,* for which she won an Oscar for Best Supporting Actress. Dukakis has also won a Golden Globe, an Obie, and a Los Angeles Critics Award for her work in theater, film, and television. Her autobiography, *Ask Me Again Tomorrow: A Life in Progress,* was a national best-seller.

E

Leslie Epstein

I don't have a general formula for driving away the blues, so I think it best to give a specific example of how I cheered myself up; it is, as it happens, a case that occurred only three days ago. Why was I down in the dumps? For the same reason a lot of writers find themselves in that territory: a bad review. Did I pull out my hair? Kick the dog? Yell at my wife? No. I filtered a disc of Mozart piano trios through a pair of headphones, picked up a copy of *Raise High the Roof Beam, Carpenters,* and, truth to tell, poured out a finger or two of unblended whiskey. When the phone rang and my pal Pinksy asked how things were, I answered, "I am in bliss." And I was—and at the memory I still am.

Leslie Epstein is the author of several books and magazine articles as well as the director of the Creative Writing Program at Boston University. His best-known book, *King of the Jews,* has been published in eleven foreign languages and is a classic of Holocaust fiction. Epstein has received several awards, including an award for Distinction in Literature from the American Academy and Institute of Arts and Letters.

Amitai Etzioni

Soon after my wife died—her car slid off an icy road—a school psychologist in Bethesda, Maryland, warned me that my children and I were not mourning in the right way. We were first angry; the proper way, he said, is to start with denial. When recently I was about to say a few words to the people assembled in Hillside Memorial Park in Los Angeles who came to help bury my son, the rabbi whispered that I need not fear speaking publicly—"Just go with the flow," she urged. I had a hard time not telling both to get lost, or something less printable along the same lines. I was, and am, angry all right. To make parents bury their children is dead wrong; to take both my wife and my son from me is cruel beyond words.

When I asked a psychotherapist about a support group, she said that she knew only about one that specialized in those who lost young children. However, she was going to help me "set a boundary." If I continued to suffer from insomnia, listlessness, and lack of interest in life's activities after two months, she could provide individual counseling. "Most insurances cover it," she consoled me.

"There has to be food," a neighbor who recently lost her husband insisted. I was very uncomfortable with the semi-cocktail party nature of several "shiva" I attended. (*Shiva* refers to seven days that people come, according to Jewish tradition, to "sit with" and pray with those who lost a loved one.) Checking with two others who recently faced the same question left no doubt that my suggestion that we serve only coffee did not have a prayer. Indeed, people brought so many additional goodies, to express their sympathies to be sure, that we ended up serving a rather lavish meal, buffet style. I vetoed, though, the serving of booze.

I divulged to those who came to lay to rest my Michael—whose name in Hebrew means "Who is like God"—that I believed in a God who is a force that brings meaning to the world, but that my belief has been severely tested. I said that I missed seeing Him in the killing fields of Cambodia, that so far He seems too busy to show up in Darfur, and that He was not shining His face on either the Sunnis or the Shiites in Iraq. More personally, I asked, with a rising voice, "How could the Lord allow for anyone to take a son from his ailing, aging father? To tear a devoted husband out of the arms of his loving wife, in the middle of the night? To deny a two-year-old ever finding the father he keeps looking for? To bring into the world an infant who will never see his father, even once?"

A social philosopher on campus, who read my eulogy, took me for a walk in the woods. "You must know," he lectured me, "that God is not a micromanager. He does not dish out specific goods or condone specific evils. He leaves these acts—and the choices involved—to us. If the good and the bad were given to us, we would not be choosing, moral creatures." Well, I did not choose for anyone to lay a glove on those I loved most, let alone send them on their last journey long before it was due. Intellectually there might be an answer as to why God allows awful things to keep happening to very good people, but my colleague did not bring me even an inch closer to coming to terms with my ill fate.

Ruth, a relative and a psychiatrist from Jerusalem, brought some solace with the saying "We are not to ask why, but what." The "what" is that which the survivors are bound to do for one another in our grief. So we keep busy, calling each other for long explorations about questions such as "How did your day go today?" and trying to avoid the immediate past and bereft future. We are taking turns playing with two-year-old Max. We found friends who volunteered to take turns spending nights with the young widow and who promised to be among those holding her hand when the orphaned baby will be born. We encouraged friends to give donations to an education fund set up for Michael and Lainie's children rather than send flowers. And we complained to each other about those who came to visit and used the time to network with other "visible" mourners.

I presume that many a shrink and New Age clergy will point out that by keeping busy we are avoiding the prescribed, "healthy" form of grieving. To hell with that; the void left by the taking of my wife and son is just too deep to fathom. For now, focusing on what we do for one another is the best we can do. The rest may be in God's hands. He seems very remote and grossly preoccupied these days. So we are left, leaning on one another, each laboring to seem strong for the others.

Amitai Etzioni teaches sociology at George Washington University and is the author of *My Brother's Keeper: A Memoir and a Message.* Etzioni is the author of twenty-four books and has taught at some of the country's most prestigious universities, including Columbia and Harvard. He has also served as a senior advisor to the White House on domestic affairs and he is referred to by the press as the "guru" of the communitarian movement.

F

Merrell Fankhauser

What I do when I am down is try to focus on the positive things in my life. Somebody else always has it worse. . . . Sometimes you need to have a good laugh at how ridiculous a situation may be, knowing that, in years to come, the situation may indeed look humorous.

Being in the music business you always have to reinvent yourself. Going into the studio and writing a song sometimes helps get out the emotion; some of my best songs have been written this way!

Merrell Fankhauser is an American singer and songwriter who has had several hit songs both in America and abroad. Due to the success of his bands such as the Exiles, Fapardokly, HMS Bounty, and MU, Fankhauser is considered an innovator of surf music and psychedelic folk rock. Fankhauser continues to make music as well as to host radio and television programs.

Joey Fatone

Well, for starters, I have been blessed with a great life. I am normally very happy and enjoy life as it comes. I have heard that many people eat when they are depressed or mad; with me it's the opposite! I eat when I am happy and I have no appetite when I'm not. When I do get mad, LOOK OUT! I tend to get quiet and ignore everyone and everything around me. . . . I just want to be alone and play video games (I find video games are very therapeutic). If after a few HOURS of playing video, I don't feel better, I then watch a movie or go to the movies. For some strange reason a good movie always calms me down, clears my head, and I'm happy again. Then, being happy, I start to eat and I gain weight and then become upset for gaining weight, then I don't eat, lose weight and get happy, and then eat AGAIN!!!!!!! . . . IT IS A NEVER-ENDING CYCLE! Guess what, I'm depressed; now I have to go play video games!!! Oh well, guess you can't have everything.

Joey Fatone is an actor and singer from Orlando, Florida. He is best known for singing tenor for the wildly popular boy band 'N Sync. The group achieved phenomenal success with hits such as "Tearin' Up My Heart" and "Bye Bye Bye." Fatone has acted in films such as *My Big Fat Greek Wedding* and has lent his voice to various television programs including *Kim Possible* and *Robot Chicken.*

Tom Fontana

I walk.

I hoof down the Hudson River Park to Battery Park and stare at the Statue of Liberty.

Or I trek through Central Park, diagonally from West 59th Street to the Metropolitan Museum of Art, then I head to the garden courtyard or the room with all the armor.

I'm not sure if it's the physical act of putting one foot in front of the other or the aura of being outdoors or the sights I see along the way, but when I get back home, I'm smiling.

Tom Fontana is an award-winning author and screenwriter. He has written for several hit television series, such as *Oz, Homicide: Life on the Street,* and *St. Elsewhere.* His writing has earned him multiple Emmy Awards, Peabody Awards, and Writers Guild Awards, among several others. Fontana has also written articles for *Esquire,* the *New York Times,* and *TV Guide.*

Dennis Franz

For twelve years as the star of *NYPD Blue* I was able to use my "bad mood" to enhance the makeup of my character of Detective Andy Sipowicz. Now that the show is over, I try to get into a better mood by going on the golf course, seeing a movie or two, or spending time with my granddaughter, Ella. Ella never fails to immediately bring a smile to my face.

If all else fails, there is always the Al Green greatest hits CD, and if that doesn't put me in a better mood I'm . . .

Dennis Franz is an actor best known for his portrayal of Detective Andy Sipowicz on the hit television series *NYPD Blue*. Franz won four Emmy Awards during his time on the show and his character was voted #23 on "Bravo's 100 Greatest TV Characters" list. Franz has also made guest appearances on television programs such as *The A-Team* and *The Simpsons.*

G

Bill Gallo

It's too true that we all experience times when all is not hunky-dory in our lives. We call it "down in the dumps." But who needs it?

Sometimes we don't even know why we have the blahs. But, if you are ordinarily a reasonably happy person, the down mood goes right along with putting on a drab tie. Does picking a gray-and-black tie mean you're playing into black and gray moods? Check yourself out the next time you want to tie that gloom and doom on. That's your first sign. So what do you do?

You start by hanging up the drab tie and taking something with bright reds and yellows off your rack. But that's only a quick fix.

What I did when I was younger was drive to the rivers in upstate New York and visit some of the best trout-fishing streams.

Getting in that cold running water with its ample supply of rainbow trout always seemed to do the trick for me. Imagine yourself in the water with your hip boots and casting a line atop a rippling stream . . . the sun is shining brightly and you are in the middle of glorious mountains to your right and to your left.

You enjoy this atmosphere to no end and whatever it was that was bothering you when you went to bed the night before is now running downstream with that fresh, cool water.

And here's a bonus for you—suddenly you feel a tug on your line . . . a beautiful trout is hooked and gives you that fight. It's you against the trout and nothing matters except for bringing that baby in. It's a good size and there will be a fine breakfast in the morning.

I don't go fishing anymore but something just as enjoyable takes my chin off the ground these days.

My biggest joy today is being with my family—all of us together, with my wonderful wife and my two sons, who I thank for each presenting me with two granddaughters. My gosh, four granddaughters, that's better than hitting any lottery!

The girls, ages eleven to twenty-seven, have given me more joy than the lifetime of sports events that I've covered in my fifty-year career as a newspaperman—associate sports editor, columnist, and cartoonist.

Give me time with my family and you'll witness a happy man, with no problems that day. You'll not see me wearing any dull ties; instead they'll be bright reds and yellows—reds to signify the rosy cheeks of my girls and the yellow to brighten up the day.

Bill Gallo is a sports cartoonist for the *New York Daily News*. Characters such as Basement Bertha and Yuchie made him a favorite among New York sports fans. He has been awarded the National Cartoonists Society Sports Cartoon Award on numerous occasions, as well as been inducted into the Boxing Hall of Fame. In 1998, Gallo was awarded the National Cartoonists Society Milton Caniff Lifetime Achievement Award.

Bob Gaudio

To paraphrase a closing moment in *Jersey Boys,* "Alone on a river with my beautiful wife and a good cigar" usually changes my mood.

If not, a brandy, a really good cigar, and the Arts Channel should do it.

Okay, okay, okay, let's get real. Sometimes, you just have to tough it out. . . .

Bob Gaudio is a singer, songwriter, and member of the Songwriters Hall of Fame. Gaudio played keyboards for the group the Four Seasons and wrote some of their biggest hits, such as "Sherry" and "Big Girls Don't Cry." Gaudio has also produced many albums for artists including Neil Diamond and Frank Sinatra. In 2006, the play *Jersey Boys,* a musical about the lives of the Four Seasons, won two Tony Awards.

Larry Gelbart

It is impossible to go up if something is dragging me down.

For me to achieve proper emotional ballast, I try to dredge up some less-than-pleasant memory, recall whoever it was my memory assigned as being the chief architect—the Frank Lloyd Wrong of my unhappiness—and then go about retiring that injustice from among my collectibles.

Unburdened by yet another cord or two of useless, emotional deadwood (piles and piles of heartburn kindling), I can convert whatever negative energy I may continue to expend on matters better forgotten decades ago, and I am able to clear the runway in a matter of seconds.

Larry Gelbart is a celebrated comedy writer who has worked with some of the biggest names in comedy. He cowrote the long-running Broadway play *A Funny Thing Happened on the Way to the Forum* as well as several episodes of the hit television series *M*A*S*H* and the screenplay for the Oscar-nominated film *Tootsie*. Gelbart is currently a contributing blogger to the *Huffington Post*.

Uri Geller

I look up at the ultimate Millennium Dome: the night sky. I think about how the light from uncountable millions of stars has flowed across billions of light-years directly to my eyes. Then I picture a river. I imagine my thoughts are like its waters; they flow though my head, swirl for a moment, and are gone. I let them go; now I feel great!

Uri Geller is a world-famous paranormalist, author, and motivational speaker. Geller rose to fame by exhibiting an unusual ability to bend spoons with the power of his mind. This extraordinary and controversial talent has made him the subject of several documentaries as well as the guest of some of television's leading talk shows. Today Geller is the subject and author of several books and is a highly sought motivational speaker.

Kathie Lee Gifford

The older I get, the more I realize that nothing gives you an immediate lift more than a good bra. I'm talkin' industrial strength. Now, King David didn't wear a bra. In fact, sometimes he wore sackcloth and ashes. And, rumor has it, he even had a fondness for dancing naked. But what he really did is something that works for everyone—male, female, old, young, rich, poor, black, or white: He cried out to the Lord. He shared what was on his mind. He wept. He wailed. He complained. He often did all of the above as he accompanied himself on the lute. (Today it would've been an electric guitar, I'm absolutely convinced.) But here's the thing: In the letting go of something—really letting go—you gain something very important, an inner peace you didn't have before. And with peace comes perspective. And usually once you have perspective, you're more than halfway home. Go ahead. What have you got to lose? Let go and let God. Try it. You might even like it. But if you're going to try it naked, please close the blinds.

Kathie Lee Gifford is an actress, singer, songwriter, and talk show host. Gifford started her television career on the show *Name That Tune,* performing the "sign a tune" segment, but she is most famous for her fifteen-year run on the successful morning talk show *Live With Regis and Kathie Lee.* Gifford has also released several albums and devotes much of her time to charity.

Nikki Giovanni

I clean ... no ... that's not true. I throw things away. My favorite things to throw away are in my refrigerator. Old, or even just plain ole ugly-looking, food, cooked or raw, or anything that no longer appeals to me, Must Go. It's a rule. I just *died* to have that piece of Brie. In the middle of the night I put on my garden shoes and sloughed my way to the store. Found the Brie. Brought it home. (1) Forgot to leave it out. (2) It didn't ripen. (3) Now it must be microwaved. (4) It will taste as I suppose sh*t does. (5) It must be thrown out.

If there is not enough food, I turn to clothes. The T-shirts that have the least little mark on them. My mother used to say that I was just like my father. If I have it on, I will polish my shoes, dry the silver, wipe the spot. Then when the T-shirt cannot be cleaned I throw it away. Socks are a favorite also. There is always something wrong ... a pillie here ... a bit of elastic showing there. Even favorite pink argyles have been sent on to sock heaven. And there are always blouses about which you simply must ask yourself, Why in the Devil did I buy that? The answer is simple: When you get blue, you can throw it away. I know, I know, you are asking, But what about your cosmetics and pharmaceuticals? Well, yes, that painkiller *did* expire a bit ago but you can never know when a pain will hit and hey! Vicks smells the same out of date. And I've never seen a bottle of peroxide or alcohol that didn't work no matter how long they've been hanging around!

So, if those solutions still find me on the downside, I pull out my big guns! My garden! I attack those weeds with so much vigor that all I can do after an hour or so is come in the house and open a really wonderful bottle of wine I've been saving for when I fall in love again. I'm not in love but drinking a vintage red makes me wish I was. And that definitely lifts my spirits.

Nikki Giovanni is an award-winning poet, writer, activist, and educator. She has been dubbed the "Princess of Black Poetry" and is counted among Oprah's "25 Living Legends." Several of her books have won NAACP Image Awards and she is the recipient of some twenty-five honorary degrees, among other achievements. Giovanni prides herself on being "a Black American, a daughter, a mother, and a professor of English."

Jeff Gordon

I've always been somebody who learns by example or through trial and error. The best lessons in my life have come that way.

My example was my parents. They instilled in me a positive way to look at everything by the way they went about their lives. They helped me realize that no matter what kind of day I'm having, somebody out there is having a worse one, and somebody is having a better one.

Having a positive attitude about life has kept me pretty levelheaded and even-tempered. I believe this attitude and optimistic perspective has been a key part of the success I've had in my career and in my life.

Jeff Gordon is one of the most successful NASCAR drivers of all time. He is a four-time NASCAR Series Cup Champion, three-time Daytona 500 winner, and four-time Brickyard 400 winner, among other titles. To date, Gordon has won seventy-five career NASCAR Cup Series races, securing his place as one of the top race-car drivers in the world.

H

Mariel Hemingway

Sometimes the best way to nurture yourself and un-wind is merely by turning off your electronics—the TV, your cell phone, your computer, and your iPod (I call this technology-free time)—and taking a few minutes to sit (whether on the floor or on a chair, with a straight spine or even lying flat on your back on the ground) in a quiet place in your home. Stay there in silence and breathe. Allow your thoughts to come and go, focusing on your easy breath in and out. Take enough time here to tune in to the quiet inside and around you and how different it feels not being attached to the techno world. Anywhere from three to ten minutes is the difference between being frazzled and finding that what your life has on offer is re-ally not so hard to handle. You will be surprised at how a minimum amount of time boosts your energy, your calm, and your self-esteem and lets you deeply unwind.

Mariel Hemingway is an actress and author who has under-taken more than thirty film and television projects. Hemingway has appeared in several hit television series and films, including Woody Allen's *Manhattan,* for which she was nominated for an Oscar. Hemingway is a yoga enthusiast and the author of a yoga memoir entitled *Finding My Balance.* She currently owns and runs a yoga studio in Idaho called the Sacred Cow.

Florence Henderson

Being down in the dumps for a short time can be a good thing, 'cause when you come out of them, you are so grateful for all the good things you have in your life.

When I get down, I write a gratitude list remembering all the things that are positive in my life. I seek out someone I can talk to honestly about what I'm feeling. And a good vodka martini will sometimes do the trick.

However, if I'm really *"down,"* and I have been, I want to dig myself out as soon as possible because it is a painful place to be. Sometimes this is hard to do by yourself, so I would seek professional help!

I also pray a lot for guidance.

Florence Henderson is a Broadway, television, and film actress; a talk show host; and a philanthropist. Henderson got her start on Broadway, playing leading roles in hits such as *The Sound of Music* and *Oklahoma!* She is perhaps best known for her role of Mrs. Brady on the iconic television series *The Brady Bunch,* but has also appeared on VH1's *The Surreal Life* and was the first woman ever to host *The Tonight Show.*

Jim Henke

Music—that has always been the tool that I have used to improve my mood, to help me get over a bad day, to comfort myself. Back when I was much younger, when I was an adolescent, I would retreat to my bedroom with my Beatles records. Just being alone with that great music would eventually lift my spirits. Sometimes it just took one song, a song that I related to because of the lyrics or the melody. Other times it was more general, just spending time listening to several songs, and eventually my mood would brighten.

Later, when I was in high school, I began playing guitar and making my own music. Though I never became an accomplished musician, I found that playing an instrument forced me to use another part of my brain, and it also gave me another avenue I could use to change my mood. Just sitting there, strumming my guitar, would help me get my mind off my problems.

As it turned out, music has been at the center of my life—and my career—for the last thirty years or so. I began writing about music for *Rolling Stone* magazine and spent some fifteen years there. Now I am the chief curator of the Rock and Roll Hall of Fame and Museum in Cleveland. And throughout these three decades, I have continued to turn to music—listening to it, playing it—when I am feeling down, when I am feeling lonely. We all have songs that have played a special role in our lives. We all have songs that, for one reason or another, we relate to. And I find that those songs are like my friends. They can transport me back to a particularly happy time in my life. They can make me realize that other people—the songwriters—have had the same problems that I may have. And so when I am sad, I turn to those songs, I turn to my "friends."

Jim Henke is a music journalist and curator for the Rock and Roll Hall of Fame and Museum in Cleveland. He spent fifteen years as a writer for *Rolling Stone* magazine, also serving as the magazine's music editor for nearly a decade. Henke is the author of the book *The Rock Pack* and has served as editor for other music-related publications. In 1992, he won the ASCAP Deems Taylor Award for excellence in music journalism.

Jerry Herman

On those occasions when I find myself in a gray mood, this is my surefire antidote:

I go to my piano and force myself to play a rousing chorus of "We Need a Little Christmas," followed by a few bars of "It's Today," and after subliminally saying "Listen to your own advice, kid," the gray snaps back to its usual chrome yellow and I walk away laughing.

Jerry Herman is an award-winning composer and lyricist. He has written the scores for some of Broadway's longest-running and most popular plays, including *Hello, Dolly!, Mame,* and *La Cage aux Folles.* He is a member of the Songwriters Hall of Fame and the Theatre Hall of Fame and has won countless industry awards for his work.

Arthur Hiller

When I feel a need for a little lift, I go to a bookshelf in my study and get my copy of Joy Behar's *When You Need a Lift* and I randomly read a couple of the "pieces."

If that doesn't work, I read two more. If that doesn't work, I visit one of my oh, so bright and oh, so delightful, to put it mildly, young granddaughters and play a word game or have a fun conversation. Being a grandfather is truly wonderful . . . but then so is being a father . . . and so is being a husband. I know the latter because my wife told me so!

Sometimes, I need a "bigger" little lift and it takes more effort. When I look back I realize that I never needed a lift when I was actually filming a movie. The lift was there. Yes, I enjoyed getting into challenging situations where I had to come up with innovative solutions, but *most of the lift* came from a group activity in a creative field I just loved. You'd be surprised at the teamwork . . . how we all worked together and off each other and all headed to the same goal. I was just thinking, "I wish our governments could work the same way."

Now if I need that "bigger" little lift, I reach for a group activity, whether it be a family get-together or trip, working with a charity or community group on a particular project or function, lunch with a few friends, or a workshop or seminar with film students.

Unfortunately I've developed macular degeneration in my eyes, so no more playing tennis, no more going to see movies or theater, and no more directing films. That's why I sometimes need "bigger" little lifts.

Arthur Hiller is a Canadian television and film director. He served as president of the Directors Guild of America for five years, then became the president of the Academy of Motion Picture Arts and Sciences for four years. In 2002, the Academy honored Hiller with the Jean Hersholt Humanitarian Award for his charitable and humanitarian efforts. That same year Hiller received a star on the Canadian Walk of Fame in Toronto.

Bruce Hornsby

Whenever I'm in a bad mood, I look at my friend Chip deMatteo's eighth-grade picture and all becomes well again.

Bruce Hornsby is a three-time Grammy Award—winning musician who has sold more than 10 million records during his career. Musicians including Sting and Eric Clapton have played on his albums, and in turn Hornsby has played on albums for artists like Béla Fleck and the Grateful Dead, even becoming a part-time member of that group and touring with them. It is Hornsby's own music, however, that has garnered him so much success.

I

Lee Iacocca

When I need a little lift, any or all of the following work: a walk in the park, a good cigar, "two fingers" of Dewar's, listening to big band, and a cuddle from Ginger . . . my French bulldog!

Lee Iacocca is one of America's most prominent businessmen and philanthropists. He served as the president of the Ford Motor Company as well as the CEO of the Chrysler Corporation, and he became a household name due to his outstanding leadership of the company. Today Iacocca works with the Iacocca Foundation, which he created in memory of his wife. The foundation strives to raise money to one day find a cure for diabetes.

Marty Ingels

For most of the truly creative spirits I know, "down in the dumps" is where they *live,* where they were *born,* where they spend most of their *time,* what they *wake up* to, *fall asleep* in, *dream* about, and have, more or less, *adjusted* to absolute agonizing perfection.

So then, Miss Joyful, the lexicon of classy prescriptions you gather from your weller-adjusted friends with "occasional down times" won't work for my friends with occasional *"escape* from down times." (There are no permanent cannoli feeding tubes.)

So then, what is it that provides these tortured artisans those precious respites of peace?

It is their very work. *Work,* the very thing that drives most "mainstreamers" down there into the doldrums, becomes the Saving Grace, the Godsend, the Daily Demerol for this army of emotional nomads. And can't we list the megamaniacs all day that were happy/only happy/only alive/only somebody/only breathing/only a person/only reasonable when they were in their "working" mode. From

Beethoven to da Vinci to Michelangelo to Fitzgerald and Williams, Hemingway and Miller, to Porter, Berlin, and Gershwin. And every greasepaint monkey from Pickford and Chaney to Sellers and Jolson, Davis and Crawford, Gleason and on . . .

Marty Ingels is an American television actor. Ingels starred in the popular television series *I'm Dickens, He's Fenster,* a sitcom about two young, blue-collar carpenters. He has also appeared in shows such as *Murder, She Wrote; Walker, Texas Ranger;* and *ER.* Ingels is a noted comedian and has worked with some of the industry's greatest, such as Johnny Carson and Phyllis Diller. Ingels currently lives in California with his wife, Shirley Jones.

Roy Innis

I come from a background where classical music was highly revered. When I am down, I usually listen to opera or read historical books. I look for works that have musical or historical themes relating to the problem that I am having.

Roy Innis is currently the national chairman of the Congress of Racial Equality (CORE), an institution with which he has been affiliated for many years. Innis is noted for his crusades against police brutality and gun violence. He was also the first resident fellow at the Metropolitan Applied Research Center, a co-founder of the Harlem Commonwealth Council, and a coeditor and founder of the *Manhattan Tribune Newspaper.*

J

Penn Jillette of Penn & Teller

Don't ever try to cheer me up. I don't want to cheer up. I want to stay bummed. It never lasts long and I always want it to last longer. I want to brood. I want to look like I perceive the suffering in the world. I'd like to be heavy. I nurse the sadness. I revel in the self-pity and misery. People are more attractive when they're brooding than when they're grinning like damn fools.

My dad was always grinning like a nitwit. He was a way-smart guy, but it was hard to tell because he was always happy about everything. I didn't find out until years after he retired that he hated his job. He hated it, but it didn't wipe that stupid grin off his face. He had been through some really hard times in his life, but his face didn't show the pain of hard-learned lessons. How could it, when he wouldn't stop grinning? A couple hours after the doctors told him he was going blind, he was making jokes. He was laughing about how he was going to hook up the white cane to the front of his car. My dad would sit at home in the evenings smiling his fool's head off, talking to my mom about how happy he was and how he loved her, and their kids and the house they had built together. My mom would say, "What have you got to be so happy about? You're blind and deaf. We're old. We're almost dead. Why are you so damn happy?" She found it a little annoying.

Dad gave me that happy gene. Even without it I never had a chance of looking cool; 6 foot 6 and knocking on three hundred bucks isn't cool, but even built like Iggy Pop, I'd still have that stupid grin on my face. My mom would say, "No brain, no pain." She loved us both so much, but we were a little too happy for her taste. We were a little too happy for anyone's taste. You know Tom Cruise bouncing around on Oprah's couch? That didn't seem that crazy to me. I mean, he's crazier than a shithouse rat with that Scientology jive, but the grinning thing seemed like standard operating procedure to me.

You won't catch me being too happy in public. I try to conceal my mindless joy. I talk too loud. I push my crazy opinions down people's throats. I'm aggressive. I swear like a drunken carny. I consume art and culture that is dark, dark, dark. I do shows where I drown and torture Teller. I think I fool some people, but when you get to know me, I spend a little too much time grinning on the couch.

Miles Davis never grinned like an idiot. What's the ratio of Bob Dylan smiling pics to brooding pics? Herman

Melville's white whale is a symbol of many things, but relaxed smiling contentment is not one of them. Jim Morrison, Lou Reed, 50 Cent, Connor Oberst—when did any of them sit on the couch smiling?

So, when I'm down in the dumps, I'm really happy. I'm thrilled. I try to prolong it. I crank up anything with a brooding downer heroin tempo: *Blonde on Blonde,* "Positively Fourth Street," "Kind of Blue." I read some Camus, with "Last Tango in Paris" on in the background. I sigh deeply, shake my head slowly side to side, and think really heavy thoughts. I go to Fourbucks so I can brood in public and hope people talk about how depressed the big guy in Penn & Teller looked over his dismal black coffee.

I know deep down inside, even if I put on "Street Hassle" and read *The Stranger* cover to cover, with a five-hour DVD of Sally Struthers's public service outtakes, no matter how I nurture my indigo funk, it's going to pass and I'll be back to my big dumb-ass grinning self. Damn.

My son just woke up from his nap. Less than a year ago he was born into a godless universe full of meaningless pain and suffering.

He's grinning like a nitwit.

Penn Jillette is half of the magic and comedy team Penn & Teller. For more than thirty years Penn & Teller have been performing on stage and screen, from Emmy Award—winning television specials to a multiyear engagement at the Rio All-Suite Hotel & Casino in Las Vegas. They also serve as visiting professors at MIT and have lectured at Oxford University and the Smithsonian Institution. Penn & Teller continue to make award-winning specials and live performances.

James Earl Jones

When I need a little lift, I plant sunflowers in my garden.

James Earl Jones is an award-winning actor and voice-over artist. Jones is famous for his voice-overs for characters such as Darth Vader in the original *Star Wars* trilogy and Mufasa in Disney's *The Lion King.* Jones has acted in numerous films and television productions, including the television series *Gabriel's Fire,* for which he won an Emmy. Jones has also won two Tony Awards and received the Kennedy Center Honors in 2002.

Shirley Jones

Bad moods? Down times? Dumps? What are those?

Shirley Jones is a singer and actress. Although best known for her role as Shirley Partridge in the television series *The Partridge Family,* Jones has had a successful film career, starring in musical adaptations of plays such as *Oklahoma!* and *Carousel.* Jones also starred in the film *Elmer Gantry,* for which she won an Oscar. In 2006, she was nominated for an Emmy for her role in the television film *Hidden Places.*

Wynonna Judd

Before I went into treatment for my eating disorder, when I was sad and needed a lift, I would use food to comfort me and isolate in, to distract myself from my feelings. Having learned an alternative, I now reach for fellowship by leaning on someone I can trust. I have a wonderful group of men and women who I refer to as my "life coaches" and I reach out to them instead. I continue to go to group meetings as well as ask for what I need. I realize now that we are not meant to do this alone.

Also, when I have feelings of sadness, I find a quiet space. Sometimes I take a walk in the woods with my pets, who give me unconditional love and healing, or I go to a quiet place that I have created for myself in my home. I have learned for the first time in my life to get with my "SELF" and ask the question, What am I feeling? And, if I honor those feelings, I find that I am led to do the next right thing for myself.

Wynonna Judd is an acclaimed country music singer and best-selling author. She achieved enormous success with her band the Judds, which she formed with her mother, Naomi. The duo had fourteen #1 singles and won five Grammys. Judd's solo albums were also successful, becoming multiplatinum bestsellers. She is recognized as one of country and pop music's greatest voices. Judd's autobiography reached the Top 10 on the *New York Times* Best Sellers list in 2005.

K

Cory Kahaney

Since so much of my self-esteem is wrapped up in whether or not people like me, there are moments when I feel down in the dumps. In general, these periods are short-lived because apart from being so lovable, I have food to shove down my feelings.

Another way that I like to self-medicate is to slip into a daytime movie, alone. Wading through a dark theater with my Chernobyl-sized popcorn and Diet Coke (hey, who's to say I am not sharing?) will boost my mood almost immediately. Perhaps it's the fact that I get to sit where I want without begging (fifth row center—okay, fine, I probably do need glasses but when is there time?) or maybe it's because I get to pick a movie without the risk of defending it if it sucks.

Besides escaping my problems for two hours I usually find myself much calmer and occasionally I get to see really good movies. More often than not, there's a message waiting on my cell phone afterward from someone seeking to end our discord or, at the very least, an offer for work, an instant reminder that I am valued, even if it's a gig way beneath what I am worth.

Cory Kahaney is an American comedian. She has had her own specials on both Comedy Central and HBO, and was a grand finalist on the NBC reality show *Last Comic Standing.* She has been voted Comedian of the Year by *Back Stage Magazine* as well as Best Female Comedian by the Manhattan Association of Cabarets and Clubs. Kahaney currently hosts a radio talk show titled *The Radio Ritas.*

Larry (Kaz) Katzman

I first try to correct the source of the blues if it's correctable.

If it cannot be corrected, I find that it helps me to get back to the drawing board and become immersed in creating funny new cartoons or new HeadLines or GagLines puzzles.

An even better relief is to cuddle a great lady.

And so to let a smile be my umbrella, to just direct my feet to the sunny side of the street . . . that "blue days, all of them gone/Nothing but blue skies from now on."

"You have a very healthy attitude towards adversity."

Larry (Kaz) Katzman is a world-famous cartoonist as well as an engineer, inventor, and business executive. His award-winning cartoon, *Nellie Nifty, RN,* has appeared in newspapers, magazines, and book collections in more than twenty countries. He is also the creator of HeadLines and GagLines acrostic-type puzzles.

Sheilah Kaufman

Happy in the Kitchen, the title of the latest cookbook by Michel Richard (chef/author/restaurant owner) of Michel Richard Citronelle, expresses my feelings exactly. Normally it takes a lot to get me down, depressed, upset, or moody. But when it happens, I head for the kitchen to "get happy" by making and eating my favorite comfort foods: chocolate, chicken enchiladas, and bread puddings.

During stressful times, physical activity in the kitchen is the only way to extract myself from feeling down. I reach for my mixer and the pots and pans and start baking or cooking to restock the freezer with my favorite foods— replacing the ones I eat during this period.

As a traveling cooking teacher (and the author of more than twenty cookbooks), I teach people the art of easy, elegant, fearless, fussless cooking. Many of my recipes can be made ahead or frozen, so I always have batches of my favorite foods in my freezer. I can just grab something, defrost it, heat it, and then *eat* to my happy heart's content! There is something so therapeutic for me in cooking and baking—from the precision of measuring, the melting of chocolate, and the chemistry that turns ordinary ingredients into a splendid finished product.

Several of my friends talk about venting anger through kneading bread and the sensuous feeling of the kneaded dough. My friend Sharon, a fellow cook, likes the feel of returning to childhood when she thrusts her hands in a mass of ingredients to mix them up. And, of course, the most satisfying elements of all are the sighs and groans of pleasure from our loved ones as they eat the final product.

Eating is therapeutic, too. For example, experts have found that chocolate produces the effect of euphoria because it contains phenylethylamine (PEA) and anandamide. PEA stimulates the brain's pleasure centers. Anandamide produces a marijuanalike high or feelings similar to a runner's high. Even smelling chocolate can slow down the brain waves, inducing a feeling of calm.

When I asked nutritionist Katherine Tallmadge, MA, RD, why eating feels so good, she told me that U.S. researchers found that the secret may lie in our heads, not in our stomachs. Lab tests have shown that an appetite hormone acts on pleasure receptors in the brain.

If scientists have an explanation for my behavior, I know I am not alone!

Sheilah Kaufman is the author of twenty-five cookbooks and has been a culinary instructor for more than thirty-eight years. Kaufman has shared her great passion for richly flavored, easy, elegant, and fussless food with thousands of home chefs across the nation. Her latest book is *Upper Crusts: 150 Fabulous Ways to Use Bread.*

Lainie Kazan

When I'm down in the dumps, I exercise. I do Pilates, I
do yoga, I run, I walk. I do all kinds of exercise; I'm very
athletic. Then I sit down and I eat a gargantuan meal. But
I do a lot of exercise first, and then I eat. Well, I eat actually when I'm happy or when I'm unhappy . . . but I believe
in exercise as an antidepressant, a sort of antidepression
medication. That's my gift. I don't think it's absolutely nec-
essary to eat afterward, but that's what I do!

Lainie Kazan is an actress and singer. She has appeared in nu-
merous television programs, including *Will and Grace* and *St.
Elsewhere,* for which she received an Emmy nomination. Kazan
was also nominated for a Tony Award for her role in the play *My
Favorite Year.* She has appeared in several films, such as Fran-
cis Ford Coppola's *One From the Heart* and Joel Zwick's *My Big
Fat Greek Wedding.* Kazan currently serves on the board for the
Young Musicians Foundation and AIDS Project Los Angeles.

Bil Keane

Having drawn the daily activities of my wife, Thel, and our five children since 1960 for millions of readers, I am amazed at the treasure trove I have amassed in my studio file cabinet. It is the mail received through the years from thoughtful readers who saw fit to comment favorably about my "work."

Perusing some of those forgotten gems instantly disperses any dark clouds that may gather over my head. Precious flattering words out of the past can miraculously rekindle that needed *lift*!

Bil Keane is a cartoonist and the creator of the popular comic *The Family Circus,* which appears in more than fifteen hundred newspapers and has continued to be a favorite among readers for over forty years. In 1983, Keane was named the National Cartoonists Society's Cartoonist of the Year. *The Family Circus* has been in television holiday specials and is published regularly in paperback collections, with over fourteen million books in print.

Aviva Kempner

For more than eighteen years I have derived much joy in keeping company with my beautiful and spirited nieces, Aliza, Delaney, and Piera. Whenever I feel the need to laugh or be amused, I dial up 1-800-Niece to converse or schedule a rendezvous. Known to them as Vivi, I always enjoy an outing with them as well as the benefit of depositing them at home.

As the girls have grown up, Auntie Vivi has exposed them to her various passions. I have taken them to Jewish religious services; Washington, D.C.; picket lines against apartheid and in support of Al Gore's call for a "vote recount"; baseball games; and good movies.

The nieces could "chill out" by sleeping over their aunt's house, where there is a special room decorated for them. One evening they all slept over so they could be woken up to watch Princess Di's funeral at four in the morning. Weekly we compare notes over *O.C.* episodes or who is currently *hot* in popular culture. We fight over control of the car radio since I favor *oldies* and they delight in turning up their favorite *in-your-face* rap music.

The nieces regularly place phone calls asking to be rescued or driven places or just looking for diversion because they are bored. They confide in their Auntie Vivi about their friends, crushes, accomplishments, and bad deeds. And often I seek advice on the same topics. I find myself digressing and giggling when I am with them. Maybe they keep me young by channeling my immaturity.

They have entertained me for almost all the years they have been part of my life. In recent years, we have had our nails done together and compared notes about how to best straighten our hair. True, during their current adolescent years I am a more dispensable entity. Yet our rapport with one another never fails to delight me. They often humorously confide in me their innermost feelings and fears that they do not share with their parents. Our conversations always end with the salutation "*Love* ya!"

Besides lessons I have tried to convey to them, answering their probing questions about their budding sexuality brings hidden smiles to my mouth. They constantly ask me embarrassing questions about my past sex life. And this embarrassment started years ago.

When they were younger and all sitting in the backseat of my car, one asked innocently, "How many penises are there in the world?" I could hardly contain myself from laughing and answered with a straight face, "Half the population since half are men." She retorted, "Well, how many is that exactly?" And without batting an eye her sister observed, "Daddy has one of them."

Joy is 1-800-Niece.

Aviva Kempner is a writer and filmmaker. She produced and cowrote *Partisans of Vilna* and produced and directed the Peabody Award–winning film *The Life and Times of Hank Greenberg.* She is currently making *Gertrude Berg: America's Molly Goldberg* and writing a book on the joys and perils of being a middle-aged woman.

Larry King

When I am feeling down, I turn to laughter. I will listen to funny tapes, watch DVDs of comedies I like, or turn to laugh radio on XM radio. I like to make people laugh and I love to laugh myself. Someone once told me that nothing bad happens to you when you laugh; a kind of endorphin kicks in. When someone tells you a funny joke, your spirit changes; there is a transfer from sadness to less than sadness.

You can't prevent being down, but you can do something about it when it happens. The secret ingredient in changing a cloudy day to a sunny one is laughter. In fact, laughter when sad is better than sex!

Larry King is an award-winning broadcaster and host of CNN's longest-running program, *Larry King Live.* King has interviewed some of the world's most important people and has been inducted into the Radio Hall of Fame. He has won the Peabody Award for excellence in broadcasting and is widely recognized as one of the greatest television talk show hosts of all time.

Kenny Kingston

As a psychic/medium, it seems I spend a great deal of time giving my clients a "lift," or helping them out of a bad mood. I love my work so much that it generally keeps me feeling very happy and contented.

But I *am* human and once in a while I'll admit to having the beginning of a "bad mood." When it happens, I follow the advice I give to others:

Don't think about the bad mood itself. Think about *why* you're in a bad mood.

Maybe it's something as simple as low blood sugar. Take a little glass of orange or other fruit juice and see if you feel better. The crankiness or lack of energy you've interpreted as a bad mood or depression might be a blood sugar problem instead.

If not, take a look at your life. Are you unhappy about your job, your love life, your self-esteem? If so, addressing that problem will no doubt correct your bad mood.

If you can't let go of something someone said or did to you, remember the old adage "The past is the past and the charm of the past is that it is the past." Don't get caught up in being a victim by reliving something unhappy and allowing it to dominate your life. You are in control of your own happiness, so choose right now not to let past anger or hurt keep you from the happiness you deserve. The best revenge for you would be not to let your past harm your future.

During appearances on the radio, television, or the lecture platform, I often tell people who say they suffer from low self-esteem to stop saying, "What's wrong with me?" Instead I suggest they try thinking, "Who's wrong with me?" It could be that they are associating with people who don't make them feel good about themselves.

Family and friends should be a support team. They should love you whether you've gained ten pounds or the shape of your nose isn't perfect. If someone in your life makes you feel uncomfortable or unloved, ease yourself away from that person. And to be loved, it's important to show love. A kind word or act can come back to you one-hundredfold.

I've always called my clients "Sweet Spirit," because at heart I believe that most people are just that. The first time I remember calling someone Sweet Spirit was with my client and friend Marilyn Monroe. She said, "What a warm expression, Kenny!" Many times, as with Marilyn, I've seen a frown turn into a smile when I called someone a simple term such as this.

Whether it's lack of a fulfilling job or a happy love life, I suggest a meditation or visualization technique that can be used to attract good into your life. This is a very simple method involving a nonscented, tapered candle in a particular color for a particular problem. This isn't witchcraft or voodoo—it's just a way to focus your attention and visualize your way to happiness. For five minutes at a time, as often as you wish, try sitting with that lit candle and imagining success already being yours.

Don't say, "I wish I had a better-paying job." Say instead, "Now that I have a better-paying job, what can I do with the extra money?" You're going beyond positive thinking—you're visualizing your problems already solved and your life in a better condition. See yourself with the partner of your dreams, if it's love you're seeking.

When I was a regular guest on *The Howie Mandel Show* several years back, I answered viewer mail using the art of psychometry (touching an object and picking up psychic vibrations from it). A woman wrote to tell me she wanted more than anything to find true love. I told her to burn a yellow candle (for love) for five minutes at a time and repeat the phrase "The man I seek seeks me." I advised her to see herself in a contented love relationship. She wrote me months later to say she'd found her soul mate and they were getting married.

Other candle colors I recommend for visualization are pink (career), white (health), green (finances), rose (peace and contentment), blue (depression/fear), orange (find lost item or loved one), and red (to contact the other side). At the end of the five minutes, blow out the candle and your thoughts. Then think no more about your problem.

The moment a hint of unhappiness starts to take over, I tell myself what I tell others: With so much of life to experience, why waste time dwelling on the negative? Choose to be happy. Choose to attract good in your life. Stay positive and you'll attract positive events and people. Remember, depression is a luxury very few can afford.

Kenny Kingston is a legendary American psychic known for his famous clientele. Kingston was Marilyn Monroe's psychic and has given readings to celebrities such as Lucille Ball and U.S. presidents Eisenhower and Truman. Kingston has appeared on more talk shows than any other psychic as well as had his own television series on two occasions. His motto has always been "Only believe. All things are possible if you only believe."

Gunta Krasts-Voutyras

My bad moods are not unlike a summer squall suddenly rolling across a serene lake, disappearing as quickly as it came. Usually the bad mood goes from somber to depressed, triggered by a sight or sound, activating a memory somewhere deep in my psyche. Something from the past. It seems to gnaw at my brain for a day or two until it becomes a full-blown, nasty affair.

I can't concentrate.

My automatic response to this moodiness is to hit the refrigerator—pepperoni and cheese on small bits of fresh baked bread (these "little" snacks start early in the morning), deli sandwiches with lots of provolone, baked potatoes with sour cream, ice cream from the carton . . . a small carton, of course. How much can a small carton hurt me?!

This can go on for a whole day, until the guilt of it and not being able to zip up my jeans brings me to my senses.

Next I try doing something creative and therefore, in my

mind, constructive. Draw a new design for my sweater business. Knit a scarf in record time. Order two tons of yarn for future projects, not knowing as yet what those projects will be.

After that fails to cheer me, I go to the library and take out a dozen books from my list. The ongoing list . . . all the ones I had wanted to read for some time. I cozy into bed at 7:30 in the evening and prop the books all around me, then realize that this is silly because I can't concentrate anyway.

The very best remedy for my bad mood is people— mingling, talking, conversing; it doesn't matter about what. Just people. I need this to believe that I am in the here and now, breathing, talking, alive and well. Whatever triggered my bad mood is of no consequence; that was the past. The present is here to be savored and enjoyed to the hilt. After my "people mingle," I am back to my usual, cheerful, impossibly energetic self.

Gunta Krasts-Voutyras is a published author and garment designer. Her essays can be seen in books such as *My America* by Hugh Downs, and she is currently writing a novel about the Adirondacks. She also designs and knits custom sweaters for the Gunta Collection, LTD, which are sold on her website, sweatersbygunta.com.

John Kruk

As a former professional baseball player who played on a lot of crappy teams, I can say bad moods were a common occurrence.

I would love to have used the old cliché "Tomorrow is another day," but that didn't work, so I found hitting something really made me feel a lot better. No, I'm not talking about other humans. I'm talking about baseballs. Taking my aggression out on a little white ball was very therapeutic. Since retirement, my aggressions are taken out on another little white ball, a golf ball. Put it on a tee and let it rip. You'll feel a hell of a lot better.

John Kruk is a former professional baseball player and a sports analyst. During his ten-year career, Kruk played with teams such as the San Diego Padres and the Chicago White Sox, as well as several All-Star teams. Kruk is the author of the book *I Ain't an Athlete, Lady* and writes the column "Chewing the Fat" for ESPN.com. He currently serves as an analyst for ESPN's Emmy Award–winning program *Baseball Tonight*.

L

Jack LaLanne

I dwell on the positive, not the negative. And I count my blessings. I also work out every day, which keeps me on an even keel. If you do this, you'll always be in a good mood. Exercise is King, nutrition is Queen; put them together and you have a kingdom!

Jack LaLanne is a world-renowned fitness expert and bodybuilder. Considered "the father of fitness," LaLanne is known for his success as a bodybuilder and amazing feats of strength. He has a star on the Hollywood Walk of Fame and has won the Horatio Alger Award from the Horatio Alger Association of Distinguished Americans. LaLanne has published numerous books on fitness and is the designer of several fitness machines.

Richard Lewis

Yes! I have finally been able to accept that I am able to feel good without feeling guilty about it, or indeed think I'm playing a practical joke on myself. It has taken me a long time and lots of hard work, so much, in fact, that to even start to list that journey would take up at least a couple of Dead Sea Scrolls. My misery seemingly started early, as I was the first kid ever to break out "with the dumps" instead of the mumps. My blood type was "very negative." My grandfather died and in his will left me "his unsolved problems." One of my aunts spent most of her old age knitting a "suicide note." After hearing that I was to do my first *Tonight Show,* I called my mother and she said, "Who else is on?" Are you starting to get my drift? My childhood wasn't a great venue to get a good feeling about myself. In fact, I almost flew to Holland when I read some experimental doctor was able to perform "adolescent bypasses."

Look, I don't blame anyone anymore, but for sure as I left home and proudly finished up with a degree from the Ohio State University, I still was sort of spiritually handicapped and believed in an "inferior being."

I threw myself into comedy and "the arts" to try and locate some sort of "authenticity" for myself. Tragically misguided, I felt that the laughter, success, money, and the multitude of mostly meaningless relationships and sexual encounters would fill me with happiness. What a joke! And I was the punch line. I was not only dead wrong with that lifestyle, but nearly died trying to convince myself that I had the answer. The early death easily could have happened, as at one point the disease of alcoholism had me by the throat and wouldn't let go. As a recovering alcoholic now into my thirteenth year of sobriety, it's virtually impossible to disassociate that fact from almost any part of my life. In fact, I've written a book on the subject. The gifts of sobriety have been amazing, and surely everything good I experience is better. When I'm in a bad mood or depressed, not medicating myself out of it always seems to be the better way now that I'm sober. Drinking made everything worse. However, Joy's book is about how to get out of bad moods.

For me, the key is acceptance. I've accepted the notion that life is really a bitch a lot of this time, riddled with disappointments and bad news. We're only human and that's our biggest flaw. I've learned that a lot of what we think is "bad" is merely a matter of perception, and we have the power to alter it in our favor. I also have discovered that when I'm sulking or on some sort of pity-pot, I get instant relief by helping others who are in much worse shape. Helping others is not just a noble and cool thing to do but it really gets me out of my "crazy head," and before long I usually forget why I was depressed to begin with.

Another huge key for cheering myself up has been the understanding, albeit late in life, that I'm my own man regardless of who I was taught I was or how I "should act" or feel. If I keep my side of the street clean and believe in myself, I have a fighting chance to get out of the "darkness" and bad mood. And as a great pal of mine said to me, "Just press the Reset button and start the day over again with a better attitude."

As a comedian, I've often been asked if this positive outlook has hurt my career. With all due respect, I find that absurd. At least onstage, I have so much clarity now, I despise myself even more. Hence, this healthier approach to living has opened up a gold mine of lunacy and pain to share with concert audiences.

The big difference for me now is that I can leave the despair on the stage and finally get a good night's sleep.

Richard Lewis is an actor and comedian who is considered one of the best American stand-up comics of his time. He has performed in his own critically acclaimed HBO specials and is a regular on late-night talk shows. Lewis has acted in many television roles, including playing himself in the hit series *Curb Your Enthusiasm*. He continues to tour and play to sold-out, standing-room-only audiences.

M

Melissa Manchester

What do I do to cheer myself up?

It's an interesting question to answer as I come to cheering myself up from any number of equally interesting angles:

1. If I am into self-medicating my angst, nothing works as a short-term "fix" better than frozen yogurt. You can go a long way telling yourself it's almost health food and not as bad in large quantities as ice cream . . . but we know better.

2. If we are into "skin crawling" angst, then a drive is good. Of course, a drive that has a shopping mall as a destination is really good. Now, if you end up shopping at Marshalls, you can tell yourself that you are not going to spend quite as much money as elsewhere. . . . But, again, we know better.

3. If I need to learn from my angst, then I'm not going anywhere. I shall take to my bed, where I use the day to watch movies about the triumph of the

human spirit, like *The Miracle Worker* (the black-and-white original) or *To Kill a Mockingbird.* I leave my warm coziness only to replenish the aforementioned frozen yogurt. (After all, it is almost health food.)

4. If all else fails and even I am bored to death with my own angst, then my personal favorite is waiting for a midafternoon hour when neighbors are at work, kids are at school, and there is only me and the birdies, the barking dogs, and the occasional humming of a leaf blower. I take my churning, roiling dark night of the soul with me to the far end of my backyard and, from the depths of my painted toenails, I yell at the top of my lungs "SHADDUP!!!" And, lo and behold, even I am pleasantly surprised at the stillness and serenity all at once inside of me.

Melissa Manchester is a Grammy Award–winning singer, songwriter, and actress. She has had numerous Top 10 hits, such as "Midnight Blue" and "You Should Hear How She Talks About You." Manchester has also written Academy Award–nominated songs for the films *Ice Castles* and *The Promise.* She has acted in film and television, guest-starring on soap operas and sitcoms. Manchester continues to write and release albums.

Ed McMahon

When I need a lift, nothing beats a very large cup filled with ice cream, two spoonfuls of peanut butter, and Sanders hot fudge from Detroit. By the way, this is not recommended for anybody dieting, but it certainly can lift your spirits!

Ed McMahon is a television host and emcee most famous for his work on *The Tonight Show* introducing Johnny Carson. His extroverted personality and laughter on the show made him a hit with viewers, and he remained on the show throughout its thirty-year run. McMahon also hosted the popular talent show *Star Search* and has appeared in several films and television commercials.

Anne Meara

The important thing is to find the best grade of primo drugs around. Do not be fooled by low-grade rip-offs. If good dope cannot be procured, the tried-and-true numbing results of vodka will suffice.

However, one has to be willing to take responsibility for embarrassing one's family, sometimes causing bodily harm to your mate, and years of repair work through therapy. Now that I am older, those infantile escapes through substance abuse no longer fill the bottomless pit of pain. It is very empowering to be drug- and booze-free, even though there is a lingering sadness from realizing that you can no longer be the life of the party.

But sometimes people are drawn to a low-profile person; sometimes they are attracted to the stoic face that hints of the nobility of suffering. Just know in your heart the most important thing is not to look for a little "lift" when you are in deep despair. The state of deep despair is your friend, it's your banner of survival, and, more important, it's your ticket to the nearest "reality show." And

I'm not being elitist when I speak of reality shows. Reality shows help us all. They make us feel better about ourselves when we watch the maggot-eating slobs clawing at one another on obscure tropical islands.

So nurture the angst, cultivate the depression, and realize that you are just feeling a lot of "stuff" that in today's market sells like Paris Hilton's old thong on eBay.

Anne Meara is an actress and comedian. She and her husband, Jerry Stiller, formed the comedy team Stiller and Meara and became regulars on television shows such as *The Ed Sullivan Show*. Meara has acted in several hit television series, including *Archie Bunker's Place*, *Sex and the City*, and *The King of Queens*. She is the mother of actors Ben and Amy Stiller.

N

Laraine Newman

Oh hell, I guess I'm going to sound like a middle-aged woman when I say: cookies. But since the glaring facts of the American Diet and the rise in diabetes have brought our country to its knees, I've endeavored to try some other things:

1. Kiss my kids and husband.

2. Read a book.

3. Play with the dogs.

4. Exercise (I know, I know, I should just f*ck off, right?).

However, the thing that *often* works the best is when I do something for someone else. It takes me out of my own little problems, and believe me, they're little compared to the rest of the world. Helping others puts my problems in perspective, obviously, but it also gives me something to feel good about again.

I'm not saying it always works. There was a time when I thought if I worry enough, somehow that's money in the karma bank. It isn't. Worry isn't action. It's taken me a long time to understand that.

That's about it, folks. My words of wisdom. For what they're worth.

Laraine Newman is a comedian and actress. She is best known for being an original cast member of *Saturday Night Live,* playing recurring characters such as Laarta, daughter of the alien family the Coneheads. Newman has also had a successful film career, appearing in films such as *Stardust Memories* and *Fear and Loathing in Las Vegas.* She is currently a popular voiceover artist and guest-stars on many television shows.

Randy Newman

Water cheers me up. Not a drink of it, immersion in it. A river is best; a lake or the ocean, next best; or a shower or a bath if that's all that's available.

Sometimes, if I'm really down, I might take as many as three showers in a week, plus the obligatory Saturday shower.

Randy Newman is an award-winning singer, songwriter, and film composer. Newman's songs have been recorded by some of America's musical elite, such as Ray Charles and Pat Boone, but it is his own albums that have garnered him chart-topping success as well as critical acclaim. Newman has also written songs and scores for several films, making him a sixteen-time Oscar nominee, a Grammy and Emmy Award winner, and the recipient of several memorial awards.

P

Vincent Pastore

When I'm down I like to get together with my friends and go out for a big Italian dinner. The heck with the carbs: I want the bread, the raviolis, the meatballs; I want the veal, the sausage and peppers. Then I want my cheesecake and espresso with a shot of Sambuca.

And then I want to come home and put on my DVD player and watch an old western like *The Searchers* or *Red River* or *Shane*.

Vincent Pastore is an American television and film actor. He has appeared in films such as *Goodfellas*, *Shark Tale*, and *Mickey Blue Eyes*. He is best known for his role as Salvatore "Big Pussy" Bompensiero on the hit television show *The Sopranos*. Pastore has also appeared on *Law and Order* and *One Life to Live* and is the host of the television series *Repo Man*.

Regis Philbin

I work out in a gym four times a week. Over the years I have found that my workout never fails to make me feel better. It is a great stress reliever and also reduces all my aches and pains. In fact, it's phenomenal now that I think about it. I know it's all about releasing the endorphins in the body by exercise, and I wish I could get more technical, but who cares. Let it go at that. Just take my word for it. It's the endorphins. All right! See what you are doing to me? You're getting me in a bad mood. Now I have to get to the gym again. Good-bye.

Regis Philbin is one of America's best known television and radio broadcasters. He has won multiple Emmy and lifetime achievement awards for his work on shows such as *Live with Regis and Kathie Lee,* which later became *Live With Regis and Kelly,* and with *Who Wants to Be a Millionaire?* Philbin has been in television broadcasting for more than forty years, and holds the Guinness World Record for Most Hours on Camera.

R

Mary Lynn Rajskub

I am in a bad mood often.

Anything at all can set it off: traffic, having to call the bank and use their automated system, having to return calls, or even just waking up can piss me off.

On one particular day, I just hated food. They gave me too big a portion, and when I order a dish that involves eggs and chorizo, I expect hot spices to be involved, not creaminess. Yuck. Surprise me with your fancy menu, but not too much. Speaking of too much, here's this new fusion postmodern café serving combinations I've never heard of . . . I guess designed to entice me, but really, as Oprah says when someone is acting morally unjust, "Y'all are working my last nerve." If I'm coming for brunch, what makes you think the first thing on the menu should be your extensive cheese selection? How am I supposed to look at that first thing in the day? That is simply outrageous. Then, there's how large the portion is. Who do you think I am? This food is going to waste. I'm not going to eat it all. Okay, I might eat it all, but I shouldn't.

On this type of occasion, to make yourself feel better, really the only thing you can do is drink. Order up a large mimosa to settle everything in your stomach. If they don't serve alcohol, or if you are sitting outside with your dog and they can't bring it out to the sidewalk because the jerk owners haven't obtained the proper permits, then yell, "This place is second-rate, pretending to be classy; they can't even serve me on the sidewalk. And my dog hasn't done anything wrong. When she jumps up on you and piddles on your shoe, that is her way of saying: I just want to love you! And what have you people got against love? You can't handle love." Then, bend down into a squat, place your hands under the table, and overturn the whole thing, grunting as if you're Hulk Hogan. But after you have done that, be prepared to run like hell. Get into your car and peel out. Make sure you head in a direction so that no one can see your license plate, and don't forget to signal your intentions so that you don't get into an accident. When you have made your getaway, I guarantee you will feel like at least a thousand bucks.

Mary Lynn Rajskub is an actress and comedian. She was one of the original cast members of the hit comedy series *Mr. Show*, but is best known for her role as Chloe O'Brian on the hit television show *24*. Rajskub has appeared in films such as *Punch Drunk Love* and *Little Miss Sunshine*. She also paints and plays the guitar, and performed for a few minutes on an episode of *The Gilmore Girls* that aired in 2006.

Ned Rorem

Soon, I'll turn eighty-three. Physically, I'm still fairly well off. Professionally, I am appreciated in my double career of composer and writer; my music is played frequently and my eighteenth book, *Facing the Night,* is about to be published . . . and I have dear friends.

But I am not happy. Indeed, can anyone intelligent be happy in our mad and dangerous world? As an atheist, I do not believe there is a reason for life. However, to kill time while waiting for time to kill me, we have invented religion, philosophy, art, love, books, and baseball.

Was I born a pessimist? I do enjoy ice cream, cake, and an occasional movie. Yet I am nearly always, as you say, "needing a lift." To work is to avoid this condition. While concentrating on a symphony or an essay, I get outside myself. And this objectivity, this "intimate removal," takes me away from self-pity and even from aches and pains. During the past two years, already in my ninth decade, I composed and orchestrated a large opera of *Our Town.* Was I happy then? I don't remember.

Ned Rorem is a composer from Richmond, Indiana. He won the Pulitzer Prize in 1976 for his orchestral suite *Air Music.* In 1998, he completed *Evidence of Things Not Seen,* which prompted *Time Magazine* to say that Rorem was the world's greatest living composer of song. He is the author of eighteen books, and in January 2000 he was elected president of the American Academy of Arts and Letters.

S

Carole Bayer Sager

Sometimes I just do the easiest things: I overeat . . . overshop . . . overthink and basically use any number of temporary Band-Aids available. But the temporary high never lasts all that long.

The next level up for me would be to write about why I might be feeling the way I do at the time, just to get some clarity.

One level higher, I try to write a song, and one level higher still, I stop thinking about myself and try to do something for someone else, even making a phone call to someone who is really needing a lift—or reaching out to someone while connecting to a power greater than myself (the light) is when I can usually help myself to get out of my own ego. . . .

A spiritual path (not synonymous with religious) really works for me, but it's hard work and sometimes a cheeseburger and fries will do it for the moment!

Carole Bayer Sager is a singer, songwriter, and member of the Songwriters Hall of Fame. Her songs have been recorded by artists such as Ray Charles, Michael Jackson, and Gladys Knight, to name a few. She and Burt Bacharach formed a successful songwriting duo and won an Oscar for the song "Arthur's Theme (The Best You Can Do)." Sager's songs have been nominated for numerous industry awards and continue to be popular.

Diane Sawyer

I have three friends who know that the world is full of what one of them calls "ghastly nontragedies."

They turn everything into funny, immediately. True but funny.

In other words, they rewrite the story as fast as possible. Most depressing encounters contain only the past, not the future. Laughter is the balloon that carries you out of the present.

By the way, curling up in a ball and feeling sorry for yourself for a week or two doesn't hurt either.

Diane Sawyer is one of the most successful and highest paid reporters in broadcast news. Her work for shows such as *The CBS Morning* and *Evening News, 60 Minutes,* and ABC's *Prime Time Live* has earned her nine Emmy Awards, two Peabody Awards for Public Service, and a Robert F. Kennedy Journalism Award. Sawyer continues to be one of the most recognizable faces in broadcast journalism.

Willard Scott

As we know, there are two types of depression:

   1. Deep and serious medical depression for which you need to see a professional in this field—and, thank God, in this day and time there are many good doctors and lots of different types of medicines out there. I hate to think of all the people down through the ages who suffered from serious depression before today's modern miracle drugs became available.

   2. Now the second type of depression I think we all suffer from time to time is the popular "Blue Monday" type and it usually doesn't last more than a day or two. For this we can almost, and I stress almost, have some fun. When I come across one of the Blue Mondays, I always get up off my big, fat tail and do something. You might take a walk, do some yard work, wash the car, anything that takes your mind off yourself. Medicine is good but sometimes your thoughts and mind come back to feeling sorry for yourself. One

really good cure for the blues, go out and do something for someone else. It is truly amazing how much good you can do for yourself when you take the time to help others.

Willard Scott is a television broadcaster best known for his many years on *The Today Show*. Scott has been reporting weather for the hit program for more than twenty years, and hosts a segment saluting hundredth-birthday centenarians. Scott is also an anchor for the annual Macy's Thanksgiving Day Parade and served as the original Ronald McDonald. Scott has won awards for his distinguished record of public service and is the author of several books.

Neil Sedaka

I sit down at the piano and play classical music, or even try to write a piece. I find it very therapeutic. Or, being with my wife, Leba, and our family is wonderful. I adore our three grandchildren. They can always boost me up.

Other things that work are walking, movies, and a glass of vodka with my tomato and crackers. Having dinner with friends is also consoling.

And then, as they say, "Just Get Over It!"

Neil Sedaka is a musician and member of the Songwriters Hall of Fame. Sedaka is the author of more than a thousand songs, which have been recorded by some of the country's most famous musicians. His song "Breaking Up Is Hard to Do" has been listed as one of the fifty most performed songs of the twentieth century. Sedaka is the recipient of numerous industry awards and has a star on the Hollywood Walk of Fame.

Liz Smith

The first thing I do when I need a little lift is stop futzing around, BS-ing myself that I am accomplishing a lot. Then I get to work reorganizing all the crap, paper, junk, mail, and incidentals that invariably litter my desk. When I have tidied up, then I feel "lifted" and perfect for at least overnight. I can go out and have three margaritas. I am as virtuous as at least Mary Magdalene.

Cleaning out your drawers and closets accomplishes the same effect.

It gives me a lift just to see an empty space at the top of my calendar. I feel just great once I load my bed with potato chips, Snickers bars, caramel popcorn, *TV Guide,* and ice water, then find my lost glasses and settle in for a long evening of no phone answering, of television clicking and book-page turning—in between the Geico advertisements. (I no longer watch commercials touting speeding cars. It's un-American for them to push internal combustion engines.)

If I am really low, wondering how much longer I will be

able to go on working before being fired, hit by a truck, or felled by a speeding comet or stroke, or if I am pondering life after death, which is always depressing, here's the surefire way to get over it. Sit down quietly. Try to remember all the ones you have loved who have gone to that Great Picture Show in the Sky. Focus on their virtues and imagine them at the Pearly Gates doing their thing. By the time you have remembered them all and thought about their special qualities, you won't feel so bad yourself about joining them. Even if there is no life after death, remember, there wasn't any life before you were born either. So what does it matter? Believe me, remembering the dead makes one feel better. Not worse.

Liz Smith is a gossip columnist who is known as "the grand dame of dish." Her column has appeared in the *Daily News* and *Newsday* and currently runs in the *New York Post*. Smith reported for the television program *Live at Five* for eleven years, then moved to the Fox Broadcasting Company, where she won an Emmy for her reporting. Her 2000 memoir, *Natural Blonde,* was a national best-seller.

Jerry Stiller

Yes, sometimes I get sad and I need a lift. My wife, Anne Meara, says, "Jerry enjoys being sad, why take away his pleasure?" Maybe my growing up during the Great Depression has left some scar tissue — "Invisible Scars," to quote a line from a Studs Terkel book.

But then I ask myself, "What have I got to 'kvetch' about?" I'm still working. I can see myself on reruns in between newsbreaks about the war in Iraq. People stop me and shout, "Serenity now. Mr. Costanza, you're a very sick man." That gives me a lift. I'm scheduled to have my handprints dipped in cement on Hollywood Boulevard, not far from Roy Rogers and Trigger. That's a lift if I don't leave them in the cement too long.

So why am I sad? After years of therapy, it still bugs me that my mother never got to see any of this. She died in her fifties. My father lived to be one hundred. Before he died, he said to me, "Jerry, you did good." He was practically blind from macular degeneration, so he must've heard it from somebody else. (Of course, I'm noodling with the truth.)

"What gives me a lift?" Being onstage. The high I get from hearing laughter is something no amount of money can buy. I've been in a few earthquakes while working the many years in Hollywood. Thankfully, none occurred while shooting *Seinfeld* or *King of Queens.* But if it did and I died, I wouldn't have felt a thing if the audience was laughing. I feel the same way when I'm working with Anne.

I get a real lift when I'm with my kids, Amy, Ben, and Christine, and my wonderful grandchildren, Ella and Quinlin.

Swimming gives me a lift. Perhaps it's because, when I'm in the water, I think I'm back in the womb during those first nine months, living guilt- and rent-free. When I watch the BBC sitcom *Are You Being Served?,* I laugh out loud. That's a lift. Stan Getz, Benny Goodman, Artie Shaw, David Amram, Erik Satie, Lionel Hampton, Duke Ellington, Anita O'Day, Joe Williams, Bill Henderson, Steve & Eydie, Ruth Brown, Patti LaBelle, Leslie Uggams, Diahann, Barbra, Ella, Billie, and Odetta. Just hearing them is a lift.

Watching Turner Classic Movies. Who's funnier than Groucho, Eddie Cantor, Jack Benny, Fred Allen, Steve Allen, Jules Munshin, Joseph Buloff, Sig Ruman, Herman Bing, Margaret Dumont, Fritz Feld, Alan Mowbray, Edward Everett Horton, Franklin Pangborn, or Eric Blore? I love them all. Maybe it's because they're all dead, and I'm not competing with them.

Dick Cavett's brilliant interviews of the great performers on DVD lifts me.

Molière, the great French actor/playwright, died in the wings. I love Molière. We talk nightly.

This is how I get off the sadness that overwhelms me when I think about this horrendous war (referring to Iraq).

Jerry Stiller is an award-winning comedian and actor. He performed to great success with his wife, Anne Meara, in their comedy duo Stiller and Meara. He is known for his television roles of Frank Costanza on *Seinfeld* and Arthur on *The King of Queens.* Stiller has also acted in several films, and has been honored by numerous institutions, including the Friars Club. He is the father of actors Ben and Amy Stiller.

T

Renée Taylor

Whenever I feel I need cheering up, it is usually the little girl deep down inside me who is needy. What seems to cheer up "Little Renée" is buying her beautiful, the-bigger-the-better, fine, *fake* jewelry. No one seems to realize that the pieces aren't the real thing. A Palm Beach jeweler who had an antiques show once complimented me on the huge yellow diamond ring I was wearing. It was the same size as a similar ring I had seen in the Las Vegas Venetian Hotel jewelry store that was being offered at $750,000.

My husband, Joe Bologna, said to me, "Why do you let everyone think that ring is real? It's embarrassing."

I said, "I'll tell you why. Watch what happens when I tell someone it is an imitation." At the antiques show there was a famous movie star we knew. She marveled at the ring. In front of Joe, I told her it was a faux. She gave me an angry look, said a few perfunctory words, and walked away. She was furious that I had tricked her.

I have a large collection of gigantic rings, bracelets,

and earrings that I don't even have to insure. Lately, if someone asks me, "Is it real?" about one of my play jewels, I just laugh and say, "What do *you* think?"

Renée Taylor is an actress and writer. She is best known for her role as Fran Drescher's over-the-top mother on the hit television series *The Nanny.* She played a similar role in the HBO series *Dream On.* She and her husband, Joe Bologna, cowrote the hit Broadway comedy *Lovers and Other Strangers* and its film adaptation, for which they received Oscar nominations.

Kaity Tong

When I am down in the dumps, I like to EAT . . . comfort foods like meat loaf with mashed potatoes or a giant lamb shank, also with mashed potatoes. Then, when I get depressed from eating so much, I call up a girlfriend and go to the movies, always something funny, maybe two or even three movies in one down-in-the-dumps day. As a last resort, I reread something by Bill Bryson (*The Lost Continent* usually works!).

Kaity Tong is a reporter and coanchor of the Emmy Award–winning news program *CW11 News at 10,* where she has been for nearly fifteen years. She has been granted several honors for her distinguished career, including the Ellis Island Medal of Honor and a Champion of Excellence Award from the Organization of Chinese Americans. Tong works with organizations such as the Children's Museum of Manhattan and the Juvenile Diabetes Foundation.

Kathleen Kennedy Townsend

Happiness and sadness are like the strands of the long blond hair in the braids that my fourteen-year-old daughter, Kerry, often wears—intricately entwined. At the thought of the disastrous 2002 election, my hands turn cold, my smile flattens, and I worry about the future. When Kerry scores the winning goal on the soccer field, my heart leaps up as I proudly watch her being warmly hugged and cheered by her friends. After negotiating a winning deal at work, on my way home I feel like a champ. Then before I reach the front door, my ever-cheerful, ever-ebullient friend calls to tell me that this time, she is not getting out of the hospital. I must visit her in the next few days to say good-bye. My body stiffens and I want to wish her words away.

The days in which sadness seems particularly overwhelming are the days that I am grateful for the length of years. One gift of age is the experience to know that these dreariest of moments do pass, that in a few hours, days, or months, life will seem better.

Over seven centuries ago, Thomas Aquinas wrote suggestions for alleviating sadness—a warm bath, the laughter of friends, learning something true about the world, doing something useful. I have found value in all of these remedies. I put sweet-smelling lilac oil in my bath and hope that a child does not knock for a whole twenty minutes. I call my pals or plan a weekend together where we walk through the woods, cook elaborate dinners, and stay up all night re-creating the slumber parties of our youth.

"Learning something true about the world" is a particularly effective strategy. Biographies of people like Nien Cheng, unjustly imprisoned during the Cultural Revolution, put my own pain in perspective. And concentrated effort to learn a new language, to understand how genes work, or investigate the history of a country I am about to visit is not only distracting but rewarding. I am happy to be using my mind and improving my understanding.

Helping others, getting involved in an important and purposeful cause is a very powerful antidote to sadness. It is not just that my problems seem petty in comparison to drought, starvation, and deadly disease. It is that my life feels meaningful and purposeful because I have helped. One study has shown that those who volunteer live longer. "Volunteer or die" is a stark slogan, but I have found great satisfaction in advocating for a community service requirement for students, insisting that the corrupt officials in Honduras be brought to justice, and working with police and probation officers in Maryland to reduce crime. When an elderly woman tells me that she can finally sit safely on her own front steps at night after years of living in fear, I am delighted that my efforts have borne fruit.

Creating lots of possibilities is key. A few years ago, I had planned a great ski vacation with my children, their pals, and two of my best friends—one of whom I had not seen in years. I had anticipated that long weekend for months. We were going to a resort where I had spent many happy days with my parents and siblings long ago. I had envisioned vigorous days of skiing followed by long and interesting walks to the village, where we could drink hot chocolate, laugh over our adventures, and revel in one another's company. We were going to have a wonderful time together. I arrived with my family late Wednesday and my pals were to come a day later.

On my third run down I fell. I heard a crack, but thought that I could ski down on one ski. Five feet later, I collapsed with a second crack and knew I needed help NOW. I watched helplessly as snowboarder after snowboarder swished quickly by my supine body. Then I remembered my cell phone, called 911, and told the emergency operator, "No, I do not need an ambulance, I need the ski patrol."

Later that day I was in the hospital—all alone—my meniscus, ACL, and MCL all badly torn. I was in pain and feeling very sorry for myself. I could not walk, much less ski. What would my children do? What would my friends do? What a disaster this was.

Then my cell rang; my agent's voice reached across the miles and the mountains to tell me he had sold my book! I was happy. Despite the pain, frustration, and distress of the next few days and weeks, I knew that my dream of writing my book would come true. And I knew that because I would be confined to bed, I could not be tempted to dine out or go to events, but would be able to write uninterrupted.

Kathleen Kennedy Townsend is a Democratic politician. During her eight years as lieutenant governor of Maryland, Townsend championed issues such as the fight against crime and the need for a stronger child and family services strategy. She has won multiple awards for her leadership skills and currently serves on the board of the John F. Kennedy Library Foundation. She is the eldest child of Robert and Ethel Kennedy.

Melania Trump

When you struggle with winter blues, it's helpful to think positively and take care of your body and mind. It helps to have a great relationship with yourself and your spouse.

It is hard for me to ever suffer from a bad mood. When I see my newborn baby boy and he gives me the biggest smile and I feel his touch, I become hypnotized with bliss!

Melania Trump is a supermodel who has appeared on the covers of magazines such as *Vogue, Harper's Bazaar*, and *British GQ*. She has had major layouts in magazines including the *Sports Illustrated* swimsuit issue, *Vogue, Glamour,* and *Vanity Fair*. Trump is also noted for her work to help others. She is a supporter of charities including AmFar and the American Red Cross, among others. She is married to real estate mogul Donald Trump.

V

Dick Van Patten 225

Dick Van Patten

When I need a lift, I go to the racetrack. If I win, it gives me a great lift.

However, if I lose, I become so occupied with winning the money back that I forget what I needed a lift from. That's my secret.

Dick Van Patten is a stage, television, and film actor. As a child he acted in numerous Broadway plays, including *The Eternal Road*. His character of Tom Bradford on the show *Eight Is Enough* was ranked #33 on *TV Guide*'s list of "Greatest TV Dads of All Time." Van Patten is also well known for his role as King Roland in the Mel Brooks *Star Wars* spoof *Spaceballs*.

W

Mort Walker

When I am feeling down and dull, sometimes it helps to pull out a book of old comic strips. My favorites. The humor is pure and simple. Great characters. Funny action. Absurdity. Nothing challenging or world-shaking.

,ust lighthearted fun. It clears my mind, cheers me up, and sends me back to work with a lift of spirits, an uncomplicated head, and a love of mankind.

Mort Walker is a cartoonist best known for creating strips such as *Beetle Bailey* and *Hi & Lois* as well as for founding the National Cartoon Museum. *Beetle Bailey* runs in roughly eighteen hundred newspapers in more than fifty countries and has been in existence for more than fifty years. Walker has been honored with numerous awards, such as the Elzie Segar Award for "Lifetime Achievement" and several National Cartoonists Society awards.